"*Sleep Disorders: America's Hidden Nightmare* is a lifesaver! Having personally suffered with sleep apnea for a number of years, I found that this book enabled me to determine what I must do. I will definitely recommend it to the police and fire departments with whom we consult."

ROBERT W. CORMACK, PRESIDENT
*Personnel Systems Corporation and
Government Personnel Testing Service*

"I frequently see many sleep problems and can only conclude that the consequences are getting worse. Fortunately, we now have this book to help us understand the shocking facts. . ."

HARRY E. GUNN, PH.D., *Clinical psychologist*

"This is just what the doctor ordered for today's health care employees who work long shifts, are under constant stress and often internalize the burden of caring for very sick people. . . "

TOM COLEMAN
Manager, Training and Development, Edward Hospital

"This should be required reading for all health care and medical practitioners."

JACK LAUDERBACK
Director, Human Resources, Vitalink Pharmacy Services, Inc.

"Now, at last, we have a book that will directly help all public safety and private security officers, their supervisors, and the people whom they serve."

DR. RICHARD W. KOBETZ
Executive Director, Executive Protection Institute

"Medical professionals all need to read this book — life would be safer for them and for their patients."

W. LEONARD FANT
Former President of the Tennessee Hospital Association

Sleep
Disorders

Sleep
Disorders
America's Hidden Nightmare

ROGER FRITZ, PH.D.

NATIONAL SLEEP ALERT, INC.

©1993 by Roger Fritz, Ph.D.
National Sleep Alert, Inc.
500 Technology Drive, Suite 201
Naperville, Illinois 60563

Distributed by
Publishers Distribution Service
6893 Sullivan Road
Grawn, Michigan 49637
616 / 276-5196
Fax 616 / 276-5197

TO ORDER, CALL 1-800-345-0096

ISBN Number 0-9635137-0-2

Printed in the United States of America
Library of Congress Catalog Card Number 93-083648

Designed and edited by Carol Haralson

The best bridge between despair and hope
is a good night's sleep.

—Harry Ruby

CONTENTS

1

WAKE UP TO THE DANGER!

2

SWEET DREAMS: GETTING A GOOD NIGHT'S SLEEP

Foreword

Our society has arrived at a point in time when it absolutely must change the way it deals with sleep. As we say in the recent report of the National Commission on Sleep Research, we must reexamine sleep "from top to bottom, from birth to death, from the bedroom to the factory, from the Persian Gulf to Prince William Sound." *There is no part of society where sleep disorders and sleep deprivation are not serious problems, and there is no component of society where there is adequate awareness about sleep disorders and sleep deprivation.* Sleep doctors and researchers have accumulated an encyclopedic body of knowledge about sleep and the diagnosis and treatment of sleep disorders, but this knowledge has simply not diffused into the real world of the home, the schools, the workplace, and community medical practices.

Optimal human health only exists if sleep is entirely healthy. In earlier times, it was assumed that the brain turned off during sleep, nothing could go awry, and there was no need to examine sleep. This is wrong! At least 40 million Americans suffer from one or more chronic sleep disorders. Furthermore, the symptoms of these disorders are flagrantly obvious. They are: (1) unusual and persistent daytime sleepiness, (2) insomnia or unusually disturbed sleep at night, (3) unusual behaviors during sleep such as screaming and violent movements, (4) loud snoring. Several studies in which exit interviews were administered to patients leaving a primary care clinic have shown that the above sleep-related symptoms exist in 50 percent or more of all patients. *Our conclusion is that "a river of severe sleep disorders is flowing past the unseeing eyes of nearly all doctors, and because their disorders remain unrecognized, the heatlh of literally millions of patients is in jeopardy."* This state of affairs is simply no longer acceptable.

Everyone sleeps. Some people sleep more than others. Some people sleep less than others. Some people take sleep for granted, while others worry about it, and some occasionally wonder if they will wake up every morning safe and sound. In spite of the ubiquitous role of sleep in everyone's life, and in spite of its inherent fascination, there is no focus for concerns about sleep either in academia or the National Institutes of Heatlh. Noting this, the Congress of the United States in 1988 passed legislation creating the National Commission on Sleep Disorders Research (NCSDR) to study the role of sleep and its disorders in terms of the health of the American public and in terms of their overall role in society. The Commission was also asked to make recommendations to solve any problems it identified. During the course of its work, which included public hearings all over the United States and several crucial studies and surveys, it became very clear that most Americans, and above all those who are victims of sleep disorders, do not have access to the benefits of sleep disorders medicine. Witness after witness testified before the Commission about years of neglect and mismanagement of sleep problems. However, what came through loud and clear was the complete failure of education and knowledge transfer in the area of sleep and sleep disorders. For example, a Commission-initiated study of American medical schools showed little or no presentation of material on sleep disorders. It also asked a number of large clinical practice groups around the United States to search their computerized data bases for International Classification of Disease (ICD9) codes for specific sleep disorders, including obstructive sleep apnea syndrome, narcolepsy, psychophysiological insomnia, and delayed sleep phase syndrome. When over ten million patients had been accumulated, it was clear that adding more patients would not change the results. Only 73 sleep disorder diagnostic codes were found in over ten million cases.

This lack of awareness is in stunning contrast to the tremendous numbers of people who appear to have sleep problems in the United

States. Several well designed national surveys conducted by the Gallup Poll organization have shown that 65 million people complain about insomnia. In addition, approximately 20 million people are troubled by excessive drowsiness in the daytime. The elderly population has a disproportionate number of sleep problems.

The root cause is the failure of knowledge about sleep and sleep disorders to penetrate the educational systems. Most other areas of the life sciences are covered in undergraduate human biology, if not in high school, and certainly almost everything relevant to a primary care practice is introduced and often well covered in medical school. Thus, concepts as fundamental as the idea that the blood flows from the heart, through the arteries to the tissues and back to the heart through the veins, in the sleep field are not part of anyone's way of thinking.

It is not productive to haggle about the exact percentage of patients who have a sleep problem. *Doctors must assume that every single person they see may have a sleep disorder.* This means that they will take an extra ten to fifteen seconds to ask two or three crucial questions relating to sleep. We already know that when this is done, enormous numbers of sleep disorders will be identified in patients currently complaining of mysterious "fatigue" problems and being treated ineffectively on a trial-and-error basis.

We also must acknowledge that there are times when each of us is dangerously sleep deprived. We are all vulnerable to falling asleep while driving or in other dangerous situations when the stimulation that keeps us awake is withdrawn. Few of us try very hard to relate daytime function precisely to sleep at night. Yet this ought to be as precise as, "I worked so many hours, and I have earned this amount of money." We are very insensitive to subjective levels of sleepiness, and even our language seems inadequate. We have trouble finding the right words to describe how sleep deprived we are, or to predict when and if we will stay awake or fall asleep in any particular situation.

It is time to totally eliminate the ignorance and inattention of our society about sleep. Until this is accomplished, there cannot be too much information and publicity about sleep disorders. Every newspaper article, every magazine story, every television news coverage, and above all, every book, must be welcomed as a step forward in this daunting task. Every effort must be made to secure the widest possible dissemination.

Given the above, we welcome *Sleep Disorders: America's Hidden Nightmare* by Roger Fritz with enthusiasm and applause. It is targeted to the general public and reads easily and interestingly, yet at the same time is authoritative. As a special bonus, it is reasonably priced. We hope that eventually it will be possessed, read, and taken seriously by every single person in America. We are massively ignorant about sleep disorders, so we cannot stop until knowledge about sleep, sleep need, and sleep disorders is as ingrained in our consciousness as information about nutrition, physical fitness, cancer, and heart disease.

WILLIAM C. DEMENT, M.D., PH.D.
Chair of the National Commission on Sleep Disorders Research
Director, Stanford University Sleep Disorders Center

Preface

Sleep disorders — which, for the purposes of this book we define as any conditions, organic or habit-related, temporary or long-lived, that obstruct healthy sleep — are epidemic in America.

Sleep disorders and poor sleep habits can have a huge impact on children and adolescents during their most important school years — altering their later lives irrevocably. Sleep deprivation in the workplace has caused numerous fatal accidents. Thousands of Americans find their overall quality of life degraded because of problems with sleep. And yet, surveys by the National Commission on Sleep Disorders Research confirm that most people know very little about the relationship between sleep and health, or about treatment and prevention of sleep problems.

This book was conceived in August, 1991 with Roger Fritz, one of America's leading management consultants. Dr. Fritz is the author of twenty-six books and the producer of numerous audio/visual programs on business management, organization development and entrepreneurship. As a consultant, author and speaker whose goal is to assist people in improving their personal and professional performance — and as a result, their overall quality of life — Dr. Fritz was the perfect partner in this undertaking.

My own reasons for wanting to see this book made available to the general public stemmed from personal experience. At the age of fourteen, I first showed symptoms of a sleep disorder known as narcolepsy. I was diagnosed in 1965, at age twenty-one. The major symptom of narcolepsy is inappropriate daytime sleepiness, regardless of the amount or quality of the previous nighttime sleep. I fell asleep repeatedly in high school and in college slept through most of my classes — barely graduating. Between the ages of sixteen and twenty-five I was involved in fifteen auto accidents due to falling asleep at the wheel. I was lucky to survive and to avoid causing fatalities to others.

My mother, a registered nurse, became convinced that I had narcolepsy and at her insistence I first visited Mayo Clinic in July 1969. There a staff neurologist confirmed my narcolepsy and prescribed the daily medication which has given me a normal level of daytime alertness for the past twenty-three years. Although I have been able to obtain fully adequate medication, I have come to learn that most other narcoleptics are not as fortunate. Most are undiagnosed or have been misdiagnosed repeatedly. Even when diagnosed, many are under-medicated.

I had founded Pansophic Systems, Inc., a computer software firm, in April, 1969 just prior to my visit to Mayo Clinic. In 1987 I retired at the age of forty-two. The company had grown to more than 1,100 employees with annual sales over $115 million, customers in sixty countries and stock listed on the New York Stock Exchange.

After retirement, I became increasingly involved with the diagnosis and treatment of narcolepsy. In 1986, I joined the Board of Directors of the American Narcolepsy Association, Inc. (ANA), which represents more than 4,000 narcolepsy patients in the U.S. and in 1992 I was elected that group's chairman.

I was appointed a member of the National Commission on Sleep Disorders Research (NCSDR) in 1989 and later became its vice chairman. The NCSDR was set up by Congress to study the status of federal research efforts in sleep disorders and sleep medicine and to prepare a long-term national plan to improve them. The NCSDR has completed its study and has submitted its final report to Congress for legislative action in 1993.

During its eighteen-month term, the commission held public hearings in eight U.S. cities where more than 150 patient and family witnesses testified about the profound impacts which sleep disorders have had on their lives. More than eighty expert witnesses testified about the inadequacy of our health care system and the under-funded federal sleep research programs and more than 100 position papers and other studies were submitted to the commission. The need for federal funding of programs for broad general public awareness about sleep and sleep disorders was one of the major recommendations of the commission.

Since legislative enactment and adequate federal funding are perhaps years away, Roger Fritz and I have joined to disseminate the available information to the general public in the meantime. Dr. Fritz presents the facts about sleep and sleep disorders in easy-to-read and hard-hitting language that general readers will understand. We are hopeful that many will be diagnosed and properly treated as a result of this effort, thereby enhancing the quality of their own lives and the lives of those around them.

We also direct this book to the millions of Americans who have less serious sleep problems but whose lives could be vastly improved simply by getting a reliable night's sleep, and to those whose conscious neglect of the power of sleep jeopardizes their health and the lives and safety of others. We believe the information in this book can make a vital difference in their lives.

JOSEPH A. PISCOPO
Chairman, Board of Directors
The American Narcolepsy Association, Inc.
Vice Chairman
The National Commission on Sleep Disorders Research

Acknowledgments

This project would not have been conceived, incubated or completed without the initiative, guidance, and support of Joseph A. Piscopo. His successful diagnosis and treatment for narcolepsy over twenty-three years ago has enabled him to provide innovative software products for thousands of businesses, jobs for thousands of employees, and millions of dollars for sleep disorder research. His dedication to finding causes and cures for sleep disorders is inspirational and unceasing.

The work of Don Young was invaluable throughout. I continue to marvel at his ability to research and organize complex material. Vital contributions were also made by Carol Haralson in book design and editing and by Pat Williamson in word processing draft after draft.

Our reward will be found in helping you.

ROGER FRITZ

CHAPTER ONE

Wake Up to the Danger!

S SHE HEADED HER YELLOW VOLKSWAGEN onto the highway, she was planning what she would do with her two precious weeks at home during a mid-term break from college. Go shopping . . . of course. Take her younger sister to the movies . . . And on Saturday . . . As she steered into a curve, she noticed a set of bright headlights approaching from the opposite direction. A semi was coming. It was the last thing she ever saw.

During the investigation that followed the collision, police determined that the driver of the semi had fallen asleep at the wheel, sending several tons of steel hurtling down the highway directly in the path of the tiny Volkswagen.

Eighty Million Suffer

Medical experts estimate than one-third of all Americans suffer from a sleep disorder. That's some 80 million people who sleep too little, who sleep fitfully, or who sleep too much. The failure to get a good night's sleep is a problem of epidemic proportions.

25 to 80 million people are affected. A poll conducted by the National Sleep Foundation shows that between 25 million and 80 million Americans have *serious* and *disabling*

America's Hidden Nightmare 23

sleep problems. A Gallup Poll has concluded that 36 percent of all adults complain of a sleeping problem. Nine percent of those with a problem say they have chronic, or recurring, insomnia — the inability to sleep.

Insomniacs cause accidents. Chronic insomniacs reported two and one-half times as many auto accidents where fatigue was involved than non-insomniacs.

Impact on national medical costs. One of the factors swelling the cost of medical care in America is the excessive amount spent on the misdiagnosis, inappropriate tests, and improper treatments administered to those who suffer from sleep disorders.

Social cost exceeds that of AIDS. The direct cost of sleep disorders and sleep deprivation in 1990 was estimated at $15.83 billion — greater than that caused by AIDS and greater than that caused by the use of cigarettes.

Loss of productivity. Sleepy minds procrastinate, avoid change, and are easily satisfied with "the old routine." In other words, sleep-related conditions tend to stifle an individual's creativity and productivity.

According to the Highway Safety Commission, 40,000 people die and another 250,000 people are injured each year due to falling asleep at the wheel. Some 20 percent of all the nation's drivers have fallen asleep behind the wheel at least once! The National Transportation Safety Board says that fatigue is the primary cause of trucking accidents and admits that only one victim out of five is a person inside the cab of the truck. The remaining 80 percent are innocent pedestrians and motorists.

The Department of Transportation says there are 200,000 sleep-related highway accidents each year — an average of some 550 accidents every day!

If lack of adequate sleep can lead to accidents involving cars, trucks and other motor vehicles on land, is it any surprise that it can lead to similar accidents on the seas, in the air or on the floor of a factory?

What about a surgeon who has spent a sleepless night? Would you like to be the patient under his scalpel?

What about a police officer suffering from sleep deprivation? Can he or she respond as quickly, effectively, and wisely as one who is alert and rested?

Sleep Disorders and Family Life

The lack of adequate sleep can cause major problems for American families. Among children, for example:

> **Bedwetters have sleep disorders.** Of the children between three and five years of age, 5 to 17 percent are bedwetters suffering from a sleep-related condition.

> **Over one in ten children sleepwalks.** Fifteen percent of all children walk in their sleep, and sleepwalking can cause accidents that result in serious injury.

> **Learning is impaired.** American teenagers average one hour's less sleep than they need each night, which can lead to impaired concentration, reduced comprehension, a general lack of attentiveness, and poor performance in class. This could be a direct cause of the decline in SAT scores and a considerable factor in the high dropout rate in our schools.

> **Up to four out of ten young people are affected.** Over all, 20 to 25 percent of the country's young people suffer from a sleep disorder of one type or another.

These problems affecting children can be made worse by the sleep deprivation experienced by their adult parents who may be shift workers, holding down two jobs to make ends meet, or have serious undiagnosed sleep disorders.

There is little doubt that the pervasive effects of sleep deprivation can adversely affect entire families, hamper the education of youth, interfere with normal, positive relationships among family members, and contribute to phenomena such as alcohol and substance abuse, misuse of sleep medication, or unstable behaviors that degrade family solidarity.

The Sleep Deficit and the National Economy

The problems of sleep deprivation extend well beyond the home. Consider their effect on American business and industry:

> **200,000 auto accidents caused.** The U.S. Department of Transportation says that 200,000 auto accidents each year may be sleep-related. Fatigue accounts for nearly one-third of all heavy-truck accidents in which the driver is killed.

> **$235 million in costs.** The National Safety Council says that accidents in the home cost an estimated $23.5 billion in 1990. If even one percent of those accidents were caused by someone who suffered from a lack of sleep, the cost attributable to that cause would amount to $235 million.

During a recent study by the National Commission on Sleep Disorders, it was estimated that the annual cost of sleep-related accidents in the United States is *at least* $47 billion.

Consider the billions of dollars spent yearly due to sleep-related accidents and lost productivity. Now add to this the cost of illnesses suffered annually by America's 20 million shift workers. Sleep-deprived workers not only require more sick days, but they are more prone to heart attacks, peptic ulcers, and digestive disorders than their fellow workers.

We have known that sleep deficits are related to poor performance for decades. As early as 1949, a study showed that switchboard operators worked more slowly between midnight and 7:30 A.M. And yet we continue to underestimate the social cost of sleep disorders and poor sleep habits. In 1991 an Exxon oil tanker called the *Valdez* ran aground off the coast of Alaska, releasing 258,000 barrels of crude oil into the ocean and causing one of the world's worst pollution disasters.

An investigation showed that impaired judgment caused the third mate's failure to respond to a warning that a reef lay ahead. Is it any wonder? The man had not slept for thirty-six hours!

The Power of Sleep

What is this mysterious state that can leave us vital, creative, competent, and calm — and whose absence can cause us to slur and stumble, to fly into states of emotional instability, to make simple mistakes that may have disastrous outcomes?

Some researchers are studying the miraculous state called sleep by examining the behavior of animals. In Minneapolis, Drs. Mark Mahowald and Carlos Schenck of the Minnesota Regional Sleep Disorders Center at Hennepin County Medical Center think it is possible for animals to be awake, asleep and dream — *all at the same time!* That would account, they say, for the way in which some birds are able to fly extremely long distances without stopping; on such flights, the birds are both awake and asleep.

In some aquatic animals, such as the bottle-nosed dolphin or common porpoise, only half of the brain sleeps at a time. That is what enables the creature, a mammal, to continue to breathe while it sleeps.

Bur for human beings, the time of sleeping and the time of waking are predictably divided: one-third of our lives is spent sleeping. Sleep is a powerful restorative, profoundly mysterious in some ways, and it influences almost every aspect of our physical, emotional, and psychological beings. Numerous biochemical, physiological and psychological things take place while we sleep. We don't control them. When all is going well, we don't even notice that they exist. But far from being a vacuum — a void — we now realize that sleep is a complicated, dynamic, multifaceted activity.

Not until the 1930s was much known about sleep. Then, scientists began to study the subject with electroencephalograms (EEGs), which measure the electrical activity of a person's brain during sleep. In spite of those advances, the ability to diagnose and treat sleep disorders really did not exist until the early 1970s.

In the popular mythology, sleep has sometimes been considered a waste of time. Aggressive go-getters, anxious to "make something of themselves" could get along without sleep for hours — even days — or so the common perception went. But with increased understanding of the true power of sleep, people realize that even *one night* without an adequate amount of sleep can produce adverse effects. Two nights can affect even rote functioning to the point where, in laboratory tests, sleep-deprived subjects have had trouble adding columns of figures or doing simple repetitive tasks. Dr. William C. Dement, chairman of the National Commission on Sleep Disorders Research, has pointed out that an extra hour of sleep each night may be much more beneficial to the average American's health than an hour of jogging.

Sleep deprivation is serious business. If even laboratory animals can become abnormally aggressive when deprived of sleep, displaying bizarre eating habits and reacting disproportionately to mild stimuli, how much more complex are the grave and pervasive results of sleep deprivation in humans?

Considering the universal importance of sleep to psychosocial behavior, to our ability to learn and solve problems, and to every aspect of our physiological well being, it is amazing that so few resources are devoted to understanding the nature of this phenomenon.

Sleep Has a Natural Sequence

Sleep is not an off-on condition like the position of a light switch. It progresses through stages, repeating that progression in a series of cycles.

NREM Phase Sleep. The first stage of sleep is called the Non-Rapid Eye Movement (NREM) phase. It is characterized by a gradual decrease in blood pressure, heart rate, and temperature as you drift from drowsiness to light sleep and then to deep sleep. During this phase, you begin to nod or drop off, but you are still easily aroused or feel that you may still be awake. As your muscles begin to relax, you briefly feel like you are floating, or may be suddenly awakened by muscle jerks or the sensation of falling. This phase lasts only a few minutes.

Second Phase Sleep. Next, true sleep begins. Your thoughts are fragmented, and even if your eyes are open, you cannot see. In the laboratory tests, your brain waves show occasional bursts of activity. About half of adult sleep is included in this phase of the cycle.

Deep Sleep. The third and fourth phases of sleep are the most restful. You move very little and you are difficult to arouse. People deprived of deep sleep often feel tired, lethargic, apathetic, and depressed the next day. In adults, the latter two phases of sleep last about fifteen to thirty minutes out of a ninety-minute cycle.

REM Sleep. The period of sleep in which you dream is called Rapid Eye Movement (REM) sleep. Although your eyelids are closed, your eyes move rapidly as if you were watching the scenes that you are visualizing. Your heart rate, blood pressure, and temperature fluctuate, and your breathing becomes irregular. On laboratory equipment, your brain waves appear fast and active. REM sleep is believed to be important in consolidating memory as a part of the learning process. People deprived of REM sleep tend to become irritable and anxious. The number of NREM and REM sleep cycles that one passes through during the night is related to the time the individual sleeps. Most people will complete four or five cycles per night.

According to a recent study by Dr. Avi Karni of Israel's Weizmann Institute of Science, people who dream during a good night's sleep are more likely to remember newly learned skills. The study examined the performance of people who had been taught new skills. Some participants in the study were allowed to have a normal night's sleep while others were prevented from entering the REM period of their sleep cycles. Those deprived of REM sleep performed demonstrably less well on performance tests the following morning, in spite of the fact that their performances had been similar to those of the other participants directly following the training sessions of the day before. The findings imply that the dream stage of sleep helps people consolidate and retain their new skills. People deprived of REM sleep learn less effectively.

Sleep Needs Vary

Not everyone has the same sleep needs. "Short sleepers" sleep as little as three or four hours a night. More sleep causes them to function worse, rather than better. At the opposite end of the scale are the "long sleepers" who may need ten hours of sleep a night or more. "Variable sleepers" may average about eight hours of sleep per night but tend to require more sleep during stressful times than during peaceful ones. None of these patterns is abnormal. However, it is also true that *most* people need about eight hours of sleep a night. Only 10 percent of the population requires significantly more — or less — than that amount, so the old boast, "but *I* only need five hours' sleep a night" is more likely false than true. However, some aspects of modern society have encouraged the idea that going without sleep is a positive thing. In some age groups and in some cultures, sleep deprivation is a type of endurance contest. Wakefulness is prized and people who suffer from a perpetual state of drowsiness are considered to be malingerers, hypochondriacs, or depressives.

Sleep researchers have observed evidence of a ninety-minute cycle that repeats throughout the sleep process and some suggest that this cycle of alertness and sleepiness continues through the day as well. Each individual has a slightly different "biological hour," however. By paying attention to your own unique cycle, you should be able to anticipate rises and falls, enabling you to take advantage of your own natural rhythm.

Modern Technology Affects Sleep Patterns

Sleep habits have changed with modern technology. While human physiology — and with it our sleep needs — may not have changed much over time, the advent of the Industrial Revolution brought with it considerable changes in society's sleeping habits. One major reason is the development of electricity and the electric light, not to mention radio, television, telephones, and other "conveniences." Electricity and transportation technology have greatly altered our daily lives. With electric lights, night becomes day; with jet plane travel, today can become tomorrow — or yesterday.

With the ability to create indoor environments that have no relationship to exterior seasons or time of day came the ability to keep the workplace running day and night, to capture a broader customer base by providing services at all hours, and to maximize the economic return on expensive equipment by keeping it in operation around the clock.

We have become a twenty-four-hour-a-day society, with all-night supermarkets, convenience stores, gas stations, drug stores, movie theaters, and around-the-clock television. In 1960, 13.3 percent of America's men and 14.7 percent of America's women were getting only *seven* hours of sleep a night. The average individual today sleeps 20 percent less each night.

Europeans have been slower to change; they do not cherish this desire to pack every moment with activity. The Japanese, on the other hand, are even more sleep-deprived than Americans. There, workers get only 113 days off work each year in total, including both weekends and holidays, compared to the 134 days that most Americans receive and the 145 days that the Europeans enjoy. The results are obvious: exhausted Japanese workers can be seen dozing off everywhere — on subways and trains, in elevators, at concerts and at baseball games, and during business meetings. Is it any wonder that the world is building up an enormous sleep debt that will be difficult to overcome?

✍ Are You Getting Enough Sleep?

What are some of the indications that you may be suffering from sleep deprivation? Take this little test:

❏ yes ❏ no Do you fall asleep within five minutes after your head touches the pillow? (Well-rested people don't normally fall asleep for 10 to 15 minutes.)

❏ yes ❏ no Do you need an alarm clock in order to wake up each morning? (That means your body would prefer to have a little more time in bed.)

❏ yes ❏ no During the day, do you often feel drowsy, perhaps even dozing off occasionally? (This is another sign that your body has not received an adequate amount of sleep.)

❏ yes ❏ no Are you able to catch a nap at will? (That also indicates that you haven't slept enough the night before.)

❑ yes ❑ no Do you find it hard to concentrate? (If so, you need to pay your "sleep debts.")

❑ yes ❑ no Does your mind wander? (When you are tired and this happens, there is no way you can be at your best.)

❑ yes ❑ no Do you have black circles around your eyes? (This can be an indication that you have not been getting sufficient sleep for an extended period of time.)

Those who have reason to believe that they are not getting enough sleep should discuss the matter with their family doctors. If the physician believes that the situation is serious enough, the sufferer may be referred to a specialist for further tests.

The best way to approach habitual sleeping difficulties is to increase your understanding and change your habits or — if the situation is serious enough — to seek medical help. Studies show that insomniacs attempt to alleviate their sleeping problems inappropriately 40 percent of the time, turning either to over-the-counter medications or alcohol. Either of these do-it-yourself "cures" can produce serious consequences.

How Much Sleep Is Enough?

So how much sleep is enough for you? How can you tell if you are suffering from a sleep disorder?

Our concern is for people in *both* categories of problem sleepers:

Those who suffer from debilitating disorders. People with serious sleep disorders may fall asleep uncontrollably; they can't concentrate properly; they endure memory problems; they have trouble learning or holding a job. These are the people with the most serious sleep disorders covered in Chapter 5. Their problems pose a continuing threat to their own well being as well as to that of others, including their loved ones.

Those with less serious sleep problems and those deprived of sleep by habit or external conditions. The millions of Americans in this category are a danger to themselves and others and are robbed of their natural vitality and resilience by lack of sleep. Throughout this book we offer information and suggestions that can help these people to deal with insomnia and other less serious but vitality-inhibiting sleep problems.

The Range of Sleep Disorders

Some sleep disorders stem from conditions inside the body and some from conditions in the external environment. Some are *associated* with sleep but have not been proven to be caused by abnormal sleep. These are the categories researchers have identified:

Extrinsic. Those that originate or develop from causes outside of the body are called *extrinsic*. External factors produce these disorders, and removal of them will usually lead to a cure. Alcohol-related problems or disorders caused by one's sleeping habits and practices fall within this category.

Intrinsic. Sleep disorders that originate or develop within the body or arise from causes within the body are called *intrinsic*. Narcolepsy, sleep apnea, restless legs syndrome, and certain forms of insomnia fall into this category.

Circadian. Sleeping disorders which disrupt one's "biological clock" are called *circadian*. Jet lag, shift work sleep disorder, and shifts in one's sleep phase are included in this category.

Parasomnias. Clinical disorders that are not abnormalities of the processes responsible for sleep are called *parasomnias*. These occur predominantly *during* sleep, and include such phenomena as REM sleep behavior disorder (discussed in Chapter 5), sleepwalking, and sleep terrors.

The lives of 50 million Americans could be improved — or even saved — if they were to receive the proper diagnosis and treatment for sleep-related disorders.

When Americans have accepted the notion that their health is at stake they have been able to make all sorts of lifestyle adjustments: stubbing out cigarettes, exercising at fitness clubs and on the bicycle path, giving up fatty foods, and adding fiber to our diets.

My hope is that when *you* consider the enormous power of healthy sleep to keep you functioning at your highest level, you will do whatever is necessary to be sure that you get adequate sleep each night.

CHAPTER TWO

Sweet Dreams: Getting A Good Night's Sleep

ne of the first notations mothers make in their children's baby books has to do with the child's sleeping pattern. At what age does the baby sleep through the night? How often does he or she awake? The rhythm of sleeping and waking is second only to feeding as a critical issue in a child's normal early development.

Although many things conspire to obscure the continued importance of this miraculous healing and growth process called sleep, it remains a constant index to our overall physical and emotional health throughout our lives. As we develop and age, certain changes also take place in our sleep lives. Our sleep needs vary, and so does our vulnerability to various sleep maladies.

Here is a thumbnail journey through the sequence of human development as it relates to sleep.

Sleep in Childhood

Newborns and Infants

Newborn babies average sixteen to eighteen hours of sleep a day, spread out in about five sleep episodes. At birth, infants have a sleep cycle of forty to fifty minutes and almost half of that is spent in REM sleep — more if the baby is premature. If — as appears to be true — sleep is related to the central nervous system processes that permits learning, the new-born infant is continuously learning.

When newborns experience insomnia, two frequent culprits to suspect are colic and milk allergy.

Within a few days of birth, babies usually sleep longer at night than during the day.

By the time babies reach two months of age, nearly half stay asleep or rest quietly for at least five hours a night. At eight months, babies spend twice as long in passive sleep as they do in REM sleep and their sleep cycles approximate those of adults. By the end of the first year, most children sleep in one long period at night plus a morning and afternoon nap, a total of twelve to fourteen hours of sleep a day.

To help infants to establish healthy sleeping patterns, parents should avoid stimulating play and entertainment at night. Help infants associate bed with sleeping. Put your children in their beds at bedtime and don't let them get used to falling asleep in your arms or on the couch. And don't give your baby the impression that he or she needs a bottle or a pacifier at bedtime.

If, after being put to bed, the baby cries, go into his or her sleeping room but don't make a fuss over the situation. Don't put on the lights. Pat the baby. Change the diaper without taking the baby out of bed. Keep conversation and noise to a minimum.

Children Aged One to Three

When children are between the ages of one and three, their most common sleep-related problems are bedtime crying and tearful middle-of-the-night awakenings. In most cases, it is best not to take children out of bed in such situations or to rock them, sing to them, offer them food, read them stories, let them watch TV, or take them into your bed. They will quiet down eventually on their own.

About 25 percent of the children between the ages of one and five experience some sort of sleep disturbance. Sleep disorders can cause daytime behavioral problems ranging from excessive sleepiness to hyper-activity.

As a side note, many childcare specialists have observed that the sound of a heartbeat has a particularly soothing effect on babies' sleeping patterns. Terry Woodford, a producer who formerly worked with a number of well known rock groups, has developed a series of audiotapes combining the sound of a lullaby with the beating of a human heart which is believed to help induce sleep in hospitalized babies born to drug-dependent mothers.

Children Between Three and Five

Between the ages of three and five, avoid letting your children watch TV or engage in exciting activities immediately before bedtime, and avoid telling them scary stories. Alert children when bedtime draws near or you are about to reach the end of a bedtime story. Resist requests for "just one more story" or "another drink of water." A bath, quiet play, and a story can ease the transition from waking to sleeping. Above all, be consistent in your habits from night to night.

Children between three and eight years of age enjoy the best sleep of anyone, yet about 20 percent of those aged four and five suffer significant sleep problems and 20 to 25 percent of the nation's children suffer from such problems through adolescence. Disturbances of sleep may be the link between childhood asthma and learning disabilities.

Childhood insomnia may cause a child to be more vulnerable to physical illnesses, may limit parent-child bonding, and may affect the child's self-esteem. Children with primary sleep problems may even be misdiagnosed as learning disabled or hyperactive.

Children From Six to Twelve

When children are between six and twelve, you will realize that some are morning people ("larks") and some are evening people ("owls").

These habits may last throughout their lives. At this age, the main problem is not sleep but establishing the appropriate bedtime. Children of this age tend to push bedtime back in order to watch TV, play, read, or do their homework.

A child who receives insufficient sleep may become irritable and cranky. Teachers may tell you that the child fails to pay attention or even falls asleep in class. The first remedial step is to enforce earlier bedtimes.

Some children of this age who complain of morning headaches may have frequent upper airway infections. More children have their tonsils removed for obstruction during sleep than for infection.

Parents should anticipate sleeping problems when children are away from home, when they are ill, or when there is a disturbing event within the family such as a divorce, the birth of a sibling, or a move to another house. Even young children benefit from talking about their concerns, however, so encourage them — but limit such talks to the daytime so that bedtime does not become a time for mulling over worries.

Between the ages of five and twelve, an estimated 15 percent of all children walk in their sleep at least once. Usually, emotional support from the parents is all that is required to resolve the problem. In severe cases, a doctor may prescribe medication.

Chronic, frequent night awakenings of children result in a severely stressed, sleep-deprived, and out-of-control family. Desperate parents often feel overwhelmed, feel that they are inadequate as parents, and develop negative feelings toward their child.

Teachers say they are encountering more and more sleep-deprived pupils, even in elementary school. The children are arriving late to class, forgetting their assignments, moving at a snail's pace from task to task, and sometimes dropping their heads on their desks to catch a short nap.

Children with sleeping problems have a more difficult time learning, are more irritable, and are less attentive in class. Teachers must learn to respect their need for sleep. Although teachers may think that children with sleeping disorders are lazy or learning disabled and may treat them accordingly, any child who appears lethargic and unmotivated may actually be severely sleep deprived.

Adolescents

Between the ages of twelve and twenty, young people need an hour more sleep than do pre-teens. The need for sleep actually *increases* during the second decade of life. With eight hours of sleep, the daytime alertness of eighteen-year-olds is severely impaired. In spite of this increased need, peer pressure and other external pressures force many young people to turn in the opposite direction.

Contributing factors are the need to adapt to very busy schedules, meet early day care and school demands, access to late-night TV, the telephone, and music.

FAVERTY VS. MCDONALD'S: A SLEEP-DEPRIVED TEENAGER AT THE WHEEL

At the end of a twelve-hour split shift, Matthew A. Theurer, an eighteen-year-old high school senior, complained to his manager that he was tired and asked the manager to schedule another worker for his next shift. He then left work and began the nineteen-mile drive home.

On the way, Theurer fell asleep at the wheel and struck another car head-on. Theurer was killed; the driver of the other car, Frederic M. Faverty, suffered serious injuries. Faverty later sued McDonald's for negligence in allowing Theurer to drive in such a sleep-deprived condition.

In the course of the trial, it was shown that Theurer had worked a five and one-half hour shift between 6:00 and 11:30 Sunday night; had attended a full day of classes in school on Monday; had started a twelve-hour split shift on Monday afternoon, working from 3:30 to 7:30 p.m.; and had then resumed work at midnight, working until 8:30 a.m. on Tuesday. He had complained both at school and at work about being tired.

Theurer had received less than seven hours of sleep in the forty-eight hours prior to the accident and had not slept at all in the twenty-four hours prior to the crash.

A jury found in favor of Mr. Faverty and awarded him $170,000 for medical expenses and $230,000 in general damages. McDonald's appealed the decision.

The fact is that Americans are sleeping less than they used to. In some cases, late night is the only time that an entire family can be together.

In 1910, children between the ages of eight and twelve averaged about ten and a half hours of sleep a night; those between thirteen and seventeen, nine hours. By 1963, both figures had dropped by an hour and a half. Today, they would be even lower.

According to a news item in the November 25, 1991 issue of *The New York Times,* when President George Bush spoke at an Ohio high school, at least a third of the high school students were clearly asleep in the overheated auditorium. College students are notorious for nodding off in class and for hibernating on weekends.

Is it little wonder, then, that 75 percent of our depressed adolescents suffer from insomnia and another 20 percent suffer from hypersomnia? Among adolescents, depression, substance abuse, and problems with the sleep schedule seem to overlap.

Teens with delayed sleep phase syndrome can't fall asleep until 3:00 or 4:00 o'clock in the morning and then have trouble getting out of bed in order to get to school.

During the teenage years, narcoleptics begin to demonstrate their earliest telltale symptoms. When awakened, they may appear to be confused, aggressive, and verbally abusive. Among narcoleptic adolescents, many are accused of using drugs, staying up all night, and in some cases, being depressed.

One thirteen-year-old boy who was said to meet the diagnostic criteria for psychotic depression was withdrawn socially, failed in school, spent much of his day alone in his room, would not talk to his family or friends, and appeared extremely fatigued and depressed. He had been told at a very early age that his symptoms were "part of a family curse."

Sleep apnea is more common in those who are overweight, and it is more common in boys than in girls. A telltale sign is snoring, because it is not normal for children to snore.

Physical growth itself may be affected by sleep deprivation that can impede the normal secretion of the growth hormone. Some sleep-deprived adolescents are inappropriately placed in special education classes.

According to a 1990 report from the Institute of Medicine, over 15 percent of America's youth have significant behavioral or emotional problems; it is very likely that these problems relate to sleep problems.

Sleep in Early and Middle Adulthood

Young Adults
In one study of young adults who claimed that they were never sleepy, 25 percent met sleep laboratory criteria for pathological sleepiness and only 10 percent were optimally alert — apparently getting enough sleep to function at their top level all day. According to estimates, 85 percent of America's youth are sleep-deprived. In fact, a recent study showed that 40 percent of our college students and young adults are sleep deprived at a level equal to that of people with severe sleep disorders.

Sleep and Parenthood

Sleep disturbances occur in post-partum psychosis and post-partum depression, which affects between 10 and 15 percent of women following childbirth. Both sleep disturbances and mood alterations are common in pregnant women and in new mothers.

Unfortunately, the trend seems to be running against young adults in the area of sleep sufficiency. A study by the Economic Policy Institute, released in February 1992, shows that Americans have added about 158 hours to their annual work/commute time since 1969. Young parents between the ages of eighteen and thirty-nine are affected most, since young mothers have added 241 additional hours and fathers 189.

The Forty-Something Group

Over 40 percent of women over forty years of age suffer from insomnia. Women seem to be more vulnerable to sleeping disorders during menopause and more than one-third of all the women in America are menopausal. Seventy-five percent of menopausal women experience physical symptoms that interrupt sleep and/or cause insomnia, leading to excessive daytime sleepiness and fatigue. As many as two-thirds of post-menopausal women experience episodes of sleep-disordered breathing and nocturnal oxygen desaturation. In spite of such a high rate of incidence, 85 percent of all sleep research has been conducted on men.

Men over forty are at much higher risk of developing sleep apnea. This malady is signalled by a particular pattern of snoring. Such snoring is like a crescendo, with each breath becoming louder and ending with a loud gasp before it begins to repeat. Sometimes the offensive pattern involves loud snorts while gasping, and with each gasp, the individual awakens, although usually for too brief a time to remember doing so in the morning. Apnea also begins to appear with equal frequency in post-menopausal women. Symptoms suggesting sleep apnea must be investigated by a doctor, as this serious sleep disorder can endanger life.

A study done by the California State Department of Health shows that middle-aged adults who report sleeping six hours or less per night have poorer health than those who sleep seven or eight hours per night. In checking back on those people nine years later, the state agency also discovered that the former group has a mortality rate that is 70 percent higher than the group that receives an additional hour or more of sleep.

The "Golden Years"

A study by the University of Connecticut, funded by the Andrus Foundation, disclosed that older people get more sleep than they think they do. Still, people in their sixties awaken for a few seconds an astounding 150 times a night. By contrast, young adults awaken briefly only about five times. Older people tend to spend more time in light sleep, and their sleep is often more fitful and more prone to frequent awakenings.

The need for sleep does not decline with age, and in a recent Gallup poll, 40 percent of the people over sixty said that they have experienced some type of sleeping problem. The complaint is more common among unmarrieds (45 percent) and in those who are retired and less active than they were in the past (52 percent). Retirees who stay active have fewer sleep problems than those who are less active.

Medical or psychiatric illnesses in the elderly, particularly those involving pain or depression, go hand-in-hand with sleep disorders.

After retirement, it is easier to take a daytime nap, and this is beneficial as long as it does not interfere with the ability to sleep at night. Recent research indicates that our bodies were designed for at least one afternoon nap a day.

The tendency to be "early to bed and early to rise" increases as we grow older.

For those who may experience minor difficulty in falling asleep, some light exercise before bedtime might be helpful. Such individuals also should avoid caffeine and engaging in over-stimulating activities before they turn in.

Depression is a disorder that becomes more common as we grow older. Some people sink into depression gradually, and feeling blue eventually becomes a chronic way of life.

More than half of all the 19 million people who are over sixty-five experience disturbed sleep, according to a 1990 panel convened by the National Institutes of Health. Surprisingly, 44 to 67 percent of those over sixty-five who did NOT complain of poor sleep were found to be suffering from apnea or abnormally slow breathing. It is estimated that one out of four people over sixty suffer from sleep apnea.

Disturbed sleep may be brought on by retirement, changes in social patterns, the death of a spouse or a close friend, and an increase in the use of medications. Surveys show that more than three-quarters of the bereaved report having sleeping problems a month after the death of a spouse. A year later, half of them still report persistent sleeping problems. The risk of older persons developing depression has been found to be much higher among those who suffer from insomnia.

Older persons often suffer from physical problems associated with disturbances of sleep such as cardiovascular disease, pulmonary disease, arthritis, pain syndromes, prostatic disease, endocrine imbalances, and other illnesses. Impaired sleep also is commonly associated with brain function abnormalities, such as Alzheimer's disease. Daytime napping is increased as a form of compensation. The changes become more severe in the severely demented.

Half of those over sixty-five experience twitching in the legs, and sometimes the arms, during the night. These muscle jerks may occur infrequently or as often as once or twice each minute for an hour or two at a time. This condition, known as periodic limb movement (PLM), seldom awakens the sleeper fully.

Older people have more trouble adjusting to jet lag.

The overuse of both prescription drugs and over-the-counter drugs by older people looking for sleeping aid is a worry to doctors. While people over sixty-five constitute about 13 percent of our population, they consume more than 30 percent of the prescription drugs and 40 percent of all sleeping pills.

As we age, we metabolize and excrete drugs less efficiently than when we were younger. Because drugs stay in the body longer, their effects last longer too. Older persons should be wary of using multiple drugs.

The Case of AnnaMarie: A Lesson in Drug Overlap

AnnaMarie, an eighty-one-year-old woman, entered the hospital for gallstone surgery. There, doctors learned that long ago, when she had had trouble sleeping after her only child began school, she had established the habit of taking a nightly dose of barbiturates — indeed, to AnnaMarie, going to sleep meant taking a pill. The doctors switched her to a safer drug, benzodiazepine.

The gallstone surgery went well. But after AnnaMarie returned home, she became agitated and irritable. Her daughter telephoned the family doctor, who prescribed a tranquilizer. Meanwhile, AnnaMarie had resumed a long-time habit that dated to the days before her husband had died. Each evening at 6:00 she mixed herself one small, well-chilled martini cocktail.

AnnaMarie's daughter began to notice that her mother, though recovering from the gallstone surgery, was gradually slipping into a state of confusion, forgetfulness, and depression. She lost interest in the activites of her grandchildren, ceased her needlework, and more and more frequently was still in her nightgown at 5:00 in the afternoon.

AnnaMarie was lucky. Upon her daughter's suggestion, her doctors examined her medications, discovered the negative effects of their overall pattern, and revised her therapeutic program. Within days she had returned to "her old self."

Sleep Problems in Nursing Homes

One study has shown that patients in nursing homes are never asleep for a full hour and never awake for a full hour. It is little wonder that the majority of them (two-thirds) suffer from some sort of sleep deprivation.

The patient's age, hearing ability, tolerance for pain, physical status, and mental health all play a role in how they will be affected by institutionalization. It is not an easy transition to make:

A new and strange environment. They must leave the comfort and familiarity of their own homes and enter a facility in which they may have to share a room with one or more other people.

An unfamiliar bed. Their customary bed must be replaced by one with side rails.

Loss of privacy and independence. They probably no longer have the independence to go to the bathroom alone.

Difference in acoustics and sound levels. Even quiet tones in a still facility can sound loud and disruptive.

Exposure to the nighttime difficulties of others. Confused and noisy patients who call or yell out at night can cause fear and apprehension in others. This, in turn, can lead to a fear of falling asleep.

Many suffer from fears. Many elderly patients have a fear of dying or a fear that someone will come into their room and steal their belongings. Such fears can prevent them from sleeping soundly.

Problems with incontinence. Some patients are afraid that they may wet the bed, a humiliating experience for them. The fear of doing so may be enough to keep them from falling asleep.

Many patients tend to sleep during the day, yet nursing homes are not set up for daytime sleepers. Meals, bathing, and most activities are held during the day. The patient who has a reversed sleep pattern may never get enough sleep.

In some areas, such as San Diego, California, nursing home regulations require the staff to check on patients every two hours to insure their safety and well being. Often, by just walking into the room, a nurse may awaken the patient.

Some patients experience pain, arthritic pain being the most common. When such patients remain still for an extended period of time their joints become stiff and sore. This aching can keep them awake. Other patients suffer nocturnal leg cramps, which also tend to keep them awake. Some have foot and leg edema, which dissipates when they are lying down. This causes urinary frequency. Waking every hour or two to use the bedpan or bathroom can severely interfere with the quality and amount of sleep these patients receive.

Still other patients suffer breathing problems, which seem to worsen at night, also interfering with their ability to get a good night's sleep. One study showed that 42 percent of a nursing home's patients were suffering from sleep apnea — but were receiving no treatment for it.

Suffering from a loss of sleep, some patients become very weak, even incapacitated. The lack of sleep can cause such severe weakness that they are unable to perform such simple activities as bathing themselves, dressing, self-grooming, and walking. This makes them more prone to falls which may result in fractures and other serious injuries.

Some patients lose their appetites and suffer substantial weight loss from a lack of sleep, which they can ill-afford to do because many of them are already nutritionally compromised from other ailments. The lack of sleep produces a marked decrease in patients' attention spans to the point that they cannot participate in activities. Many then become apathetic about their appearance and health and are on a downward spiral.

Some patients withdraw from groups and activities in an expression of depression. They are melancholy and often preoccupied with unhappy thoughts. Many will talk about not wanting to live or about being in a hopeless situation.

Some may have extended periods when they do not know where they are and cannot identify time. They may take a short daytime nap and wake up thinking it is morning, or wake up at night after only two or three hours of sleep and dress, thinking it is breakfast time. Some other patients become agitated, which can manifest itself by noisiness, restlessness, purposeless movements, and in severe cases, physical aggression toward staff and other patients. This condition, known as "sundowning," occurs in 12 to 20 percent of the nation's demented patients.

Sleeping pills are not recommended for the elderly, in most cases. Many elderly people react very strongly to medications, because the current strength and dose recommendations for sleeping pills were not established with the frail or elderly individual in mind.

Elderly patients who take sleeping pills at night often are stuporous in the morning. The side effects often are psychological in nature, making it difficult to determine whether behavior problems are caused by a lack of sleep or by the medication itself.

Another serious caution about the long-term use of sleeping pills is that it can result in the patient either developing a tolerance for the medication or becoming addicted to it.

When Should You Seek Help?

✍ Sleep Symptom Quiz

Check Yes beside the statements below that describe symptoms you have had in the past year and No beside those that do not. Count the number of Yes checkmarks, then look at the explanation provided below.

❏ yes ❏ no 1. Falling asleep is hard for me.

❏ yes ❏ no 2. I have too much on my mind to go to sleep.

❏ yes ❏ no 3. When I wake up in the night, I can't go back to sleep.

❏ yes ❏ no 4. I can't relax because I have too many worries.

❏ yes ❏ no 5. Although I sleep all night, I'm tired in the morning.

❏ yes ❏ no 6. Sometimes I'm afraid to close my eyes and go to sleep.

❏ yes ❏ no 7. I wake up too early.

❏ yes ❏ no 8. It takes me more than an hour or so to fall asleep.

❏ yes ❏ no 9. I am stiff and sore in the morning.

❏ yes ❏ no 10. I feel depressed when I can't sleep.

Even if you have checked Yes only once, you may want to consult your doctor if you are concerned about this problem. If you have checked Yes for:

*1 to 3 statements - You may not have a problem. Be assured that it is not unusual to have trouble sleeping at some point in your life.

*4 to 6 statements - You may have a problem. Making the changes recommended below may help. If not, talk with your doctor.

*7 to 10 statements - You may have a sleep problem that requires medical attention.

✍ Guilty or Not Guilty? Simple Changes May Help

Often, simple changes in daily routine can improve sleep. Assess your own sleep-related habits. Do you:

❑ yes ❑ no **Avoid caffeine within six hours of bedtime?**

❑ yes ❑ no **Avoid alcohol and smoking within one to two hours of bedtime?**

❑ yes ❑ no **Exercise regularly?** Get vigorous exercise in the late afternoon. Strenuous exercise before sleep may actually impair your ability to sleep.

❑ yes ❑ no **Nap?** Resting during the day may be necessary for some people, but daytime naps can interfere with nighttime sleep. Sleep scientists have observed that daytime sleep does not show the same brain wave patterns as night sleep. REM sleep, for example occupied a third of the morning nap time but scarcely appeared in the sleep of afternoon nappers. Afternoon and evening naps were predominantly deep-stage sleep, which may explain why evening naps leave many people feeling loggy.

❑ yes ❑ no **Have a relaxing presleep ritual?** If not, try taking a warm bath or reading for a few minutes at bedtime.

❑ yes ❑ no **Go to bed only when you are sleepy?** Use your bed for sleep only, not as an office or a place to watch television.

❑ yes ❑ no **Get up at about the same time every day, regardless of when you fall asleep?** A regular rising hour contributes to healthy sleep.

❑ yes ❑ no **Worry at bedtime? Instead, dedicate a specific time for addressing your concerns.** Select a time — perhaps thirty minutes after dinner — for writing down problems and possible solutions. Then leave them on the page; don't take them to bed with you.

❑ yes ❑ no **Stay in bed fretting when you can't sleep?** After ten to fifteen minutes, go to another room and read or watch television until you feel sleepy.

The Importance of Asking for Help

It's important to ask for help if you are having sleep problems. You should consider getting medical advice if your sleep has been disturbed at least several times over the past month, or if sleep problems interfere with the way you feel or function during the day. Your doctor will evaluate your general health and ask about your usual sleep habits. Sometimes, all that is needed is helpful advice. Better sleep habits, exercise, and attitude can often take care of the problem. Your physician may recommend that you go to a sleep center to have your sleep evaluated by specialists. They may wish to monitor you while you sleep to identify problems and point to treatment options.

When used appropriately, sleep medications can provide relief for some types of insomnia. They may be especially useful in improving sleep over the short run, such as during stressful periods or through changes in your work schedule.

Try Keeping a Log

But good sleep habits play by far the most important role in ensuring good sleep. Keeping a sleep log for a week or two often identifies trouble spots. Specify when you go to bed, when you get up, at what hour you drink caffeine-containing beverages or alcohol, and when and how much you exercise.

CHAPTER THREE

Lights Out: How The Sleep Problem Costs Us All

hat do the grounding of the *Exxon Valdez*, the *Challenger* disaster, the grounding of the *World Prodigy*, the near-catastrophe at Three-Mile Island, the catastrophe at Chernobyl, and the Union Carbide explosion in Bhopal have in common?

Read on and find out.

Exxon Valdez: Crude Oil Spill Decimates the Ecology of Prince William Sound

At about midnight on March 24, 1989, the tanker *Exxon Valdez*, loaded with almost 1.3 million barrels of crude oil, ran aground on Bligh Reef in Prince William Sound in Alaska. About 258,000 barrels of oil spilled into the ocean. The cost:

In lost cargo — **$3.4 million**

In damage to the vessel — **$25 million**

The clean-up operation in 1989 — **$1.85 billion**

Lost patronage to Exxon due to customer protests — **untold**

Lost marine animals — **in the thousands**

The subsequent investigation by the National Transportation Safety Board (NTSB) found that the captain of the ship had gone below decks and quite likely was drunk at the time of the accident, but that did he not *cause* the accident. The culprits that actually caused the disaster: *There were no rested deck officers available to stand watch while the ship sailed through Prince William Sound* — or, as the report read, "Failure of the third mate to properly maneuver the vessel [resulted from] fatigue and excessive workload."

The NTSB discovered that the third mate, who was alone on the bridge at the time of the accident, had engaged in physically demanding activities on the day of the accident and on the day before that. He had slept for as little as four hours during the night previous to the accident, even though he had also taken a short nap in the afternoon. The accident took place at midnight, a low point in the circadian cycle — a naturally occurring period of low alertness.

Exxon vessels normally have two officers on duty in such situations, one to navigate the ship and one to plot the course. In this case, however, the third mate was alone because the master was impaired from the consumption of alcohol. Sleep deprivation interacts strongly with alcohol and substance abuse.

The third mate, himself badly deprived of sleep, had a window of six minutes in which he should have perceived the ship's danger and made a corrective change in its course. He failed to take appropriate action on two separate occasions.

It is entirely possible that the third mate experienced micro-sleep periods during those vital six minutes in which he said that he was plotting his course. Such brief episodes of sleep have been observed often in airline pilots and train engineers, both of whom also frequently work on night shifts.

The NTSB determined that Exxon Shipping had work policies that created conditions conducive to fatigue among tanker crews. As a matter of fact, it learned that it is common in the marine industry for officers aboard merchant vessels to sleep unusual hours, relieving each other after six-hour shifts. The NTSB recommended that such policies be changed and also recommended that the U.S. Coast Guard develop a means to enforce the rule that officers on watch during departures from port must be sufficiently rested.

The NTSB reiterated previous recommendations to the Department of Transportation to:

> **Research.** Expedite research programs to study the effects of fatigue, sleep loss, and circadian factors on transportation system safety.

> **Inform.** Disseminate information and educational material to transportation industry personnel and management regarding shift work, work-and-rest schedules, and proper regimens of health, diet and rest.

> **Review regulations.** Review and upgrade regulations governing hours of service for all transportation modes to assure that they are consistent and that they incorporate the results of the latest research on fatigue and sleep issues.

To quote the NTSB report: "Poor scheduling of work and rest time continues to affect the performance of operating personnel in virtually all modes of transportation. It appears that, with minor exceptions, neither management nor the labor segments of the transportation industry properly considers the adverse effects of irregular and unpredictable cycles of work and rest on its vehicle-operating personnel."

World Prodigy: A Grounded Tanker Soaks Narragansett Bay with Oil

A less well-publicized incident occurred on June 23, 1989, almost three months to the day following the *Exxon Valdez* disaster. In this incident, the *World Prodigy,* a Greek tanker en route from Burgas, Bulgaria to Providence, Rhode Island was grounded on Brenton Reef in the Rhode Island Sound. Of the 195,000 barrels of diesel oil aboard the ship, 7,000 barrels were spilled into the waters of the sound and into Narragansett Bay.

Fortunately, there were no deaths or injuries, and much of the oil evaporated, minimizing the damage to the environment.

Once again, the National Transportation Safety Board conducted an investigation, and once again the finding was that the probable cause of the accident was the master's impaired judgment due to acute fatigue.

The master had been on duty in excess of thirty-three hours at the time the ship grounded.

Damage to the vessel was $1 million.

The *Challenger* Space Shuttle Tragedy

Following the terrible tragedy aboard the *Challenger* space shuttle on January 28, 1986, numerous investigations were launched. After all, seven astronauts had died and the entire world had witnessed the tragic event over and over again on TV.

One of these investigations centered on the condition of the ground crews who were involved in the launch. The personnel under investigation were employees of two large contractors, Lockheed Space Operations Company and Morton Thiokol.

In the report of the Presidential Commission on the Space Shuttle *Challenger* Accident, these findings were disclosed:

Five aborts and two launches preceded in the same month.
During the month of January, the month in which the

accident occurred, the employees already had participated in five aborts and two launches, of which three events occurred on Saturday, Sunday and Monday.

Exceptionally high overtime was accrued immediately before the accident. During the three-month period preceding the accident on January 28, the various operating components at Kennedy reported an exceptionally high level of overtime.

In reporting overtime at Kennedy, a figure of 20 percent is the equivalent of a forty-eight-hour or six-day workweek. Some Kennedy units were reporting overtime in the 27.7 percent range at that time. Many others reported overtime in the 20 to 26 percent range; i.e., the equivalent of forty-eight- to fifty-hour work weeks.

Some individual examples of the excessive workload being borne by Lockheed and Morton Thiokol employees at the time of the *Challenger* disaster:

A mechanical technician team leader had averaged over eighty hours a week. This man, whose shift began at 8:00 A.M., had often worked until midnight. In almost a month, this employee had worked only two standard eight-hour days.

An electronic technician had worked twenty-three consecutive days without a day off. This man worked the third shift beginning at midnight. Immediately preceding the *Challenger* accident, he worked twenty-three consecutive days, more than half of them over eleven hours long. Then, after two days off, he worked another forty-four days in a row, including twenty-nine days over eleven hours long, seven twelve-hour days, and two fifteen-hour days!

A manager of the technical shops had worked twenty-six consecutive days, many twelve hours or more. This manager worked twenty-six consecutive days on the second shift, including seventeen days that were twelve hours long or longer. During the month of January, he continued to work on the same shift for another twenty-six consecutive days, including eighteen days that were of twelve hours' duration or more. He worked for twelve hours or more on sixteen consecutive days!

A lead electrician had worked fifty consecutive days on the third shift — midnight to 8:00 A.M. This man worked more consecutive days than anyone studied in the Lockheed sample. On well over half of these days, the man continued to work until noon!

Over the period under study, *the twenty-hour limit on overtime was exceeded 480 times by employees of Morton Thiokol and 2,512 times by Lockheed employees.* People who are as fatigued as those individuals are generally error-prone, but there is no system for monitoring overtime work at Kennedy from a safety perspective.

A Lockheed Incident/Error Review Board looked at a total of 117 incidents for calendar year 1984 and 147 incidents for calendar year 1985. In their terminology, an incident is a mishap in which the property damage is less than $25,000. Of those incidents, 51.3 percent and 56.5 percent, respectively, were attributable to some type of human error. There also were twelve reportable mishaps in 1984 and twenty-four mishaps in 1985 in which the property damage was greater than $25,000.

Three-Mile Island, Bhopal, Chernobyl: Nighttime Disasters

A series of breakdowns in the cooling system of the Three Mile Island nuclear power plant near Harrisburg, Pennsylvania, led to a major nuclear accident on March 28, 1979. The Nuclear Regulatory Commission (NRC) warned of a possible core meltdown and pregnant women and preschool children were advised to leave the area. It took one harrowing week to stabilize the plant. The catastrophic results of a meltdown were averted although some radiation had been released into the air and the plant was seriously crippled. The sequence of events began at 4:00 in the morning.

A gas leak occurred at a pesticide plant owned by Union Carbide and operated in the central Indian city of Bhopal on December 3, 1984. A night breeze swept the deadly gases through nearby densely populated areas where residents lay sleeping. Nearly 2,000 people died and 50,000 more were were injured. The state government filed a negligence suit against Union Carbide asking for $1 billion in damages. The accident occurred on the night shift.

On April 26, 1986, the world's most devastating nuclear disaster occurred at Chernobyl, Ukraine in Soviet Russia. Many died and a great number more were affected by radiation likely to later produce cancers, birth defects, miscarriages. The accident was judged to have been caused by human error; it occurred in the early hours of the morning.

A Lesson Learned?

So what do these immensely destructive events, with their shocking toll on human life and other resources have in common? *There is a very real possibility that each one of those horrifying events occurred, entirely or in part, because the personnel involved were victims of sleep deprivation.*

There were 111 nuclear power reactors licensed for operation by the NRC in 1989 and five additional reactors are scheduled to be completed by 1995. Perhaps by that time the nation will have learned the hazards of shift work, the importance of allowing sleep-stressed employees to take occasional naps, and the benefits of getting an adequate amount of sleep each night.

Police Officers and Fire Fighters

Both police officers and fire fighters are called upon to do shift work. Like people employed in the health care field, people in these career fields are required to work around the clock seven days a week. Yet, as we have already seen, shift work involves inherent dangers from fatigue, impaired judgment, slowed reaction time, and a lessening of other mental and physical facilities because of sleep deprivation. It has been documented, for example, that most police officers are killed between 8:00 P.M. and 4:00 A.M.

Obviously, society needs the services of the people who do this difficult work — and the need doesn't go away just because the sun goes down. However, while still providing round-the-clock protection to their citizens, some cities have begun to give wiser consideration to human sleep needs when structuring the schedules of those who perform these protective services. Take, for example, the Philadelphia police department.

In 1983, the Philadelphia police department was working on a four-platoon work schedule involving eight-hour days, with six days on and two days off. Under this schedule:

Officers reported sleep problems. Half of the officers reported a poor quality of sleep. Eighty percent reported falling asleep at least once a week while on the night shift.

One-quarter had or nearly had accidents. Twenty-five percent of the officers reported being in auto accidents or near-misses during the previous year due to sleepiness.

Three-quarters reported family disharmony. Over 75 percent said that their families were dissatisfied with their work schedules.

More than one-third required a week or more to adjust to

shift change. Thity-five percent took either an entire week to adjust to a shift rotation or never did adjust fully.

Recognizing the severity of these problems, the department changed to a three-platoon system involving an eight-and-one-half-hour day, with four days on and two days off. It also instituted a plan for proportional staffing so that the number of officers on duty matched the number of calls received. The maximum number of consecutive workdays was reduced from six to four; the average work week lowered from forty hours to just under forty; the average workdays per year dropped from 261 to 244; the days off increased from 104 to 121; and the number of weekend days off rose from thirty to thirty-four or thirty-five.

Under the new schedule:

> **Sleep complaints decreased.** There was a fourfold decrease in the number of complaints about poor sleep. Twice as many said that they had no daytime sleepiness.

> **Sleeping on the job decreased.** The number of incidents of sleeping on the job dropped. The level of alertness improved on the night shift.

> **Accidents declined.** There was a decline in the number of on-the-job accidents per mile driven.

> **Use of depressants declined.** There was a reduction in the use of sleeping pills and alcohol.

> **Family harmony improved.** Families were five times more satisfied with the work schedule.

Philadelphia should be complimented on its far-sightedness. It is a frightening thing to think about armed police officers or harried firemen making life-and-death decisions when their minds are sluggish from the loss of sleep.

Airborne Security: Let Pilots Maximize Alertness

Jet lag is an ongoing problem for the crews on international routes (see the discussion of jet lag in Chapter Three). Air crews regularly fly rapid sequences across multiple time zones, work irregular hours, and sleep on unusual schedules.

One airline pilot admitted that "There have been times I've been so sleepy I was nodding off as we were taxiing to get into takeoff position."

Because most of the maintenance examinations on aircraft are conducted at night so that the planes will be available for scheduled flights during the day, the consequences of night (shift) work may also become a factor in the safety of air travel.

Field and laboratory research being conducted by the Aviation Human Factors Branch at the National Aeronautics and Space Administration's Ames Research Center soon may pave the way for crews to take restorative naps on long flights. FAA regulations governing flight operations have forbidden napping in the cockpit for many years, but NASA is developing irrefutable evidence that rotating cockpit naps during times of minimal demand can result in a significant increase in personnel performance. A two-year study showed that pilots who were allowed to snooze for forty minutes while their co-pilots took command of the aircraft did better on vigilance tests than those who were not allowed to take a sleep break.

On the Rails: Asleep at the Throttle

In 1984, two Burlington Northern trains collided, killing five crew members and injuring two. Damages amounted to $3.9 million. The probable cause: the engineer on one train fell asleep.

In January, 1988, a fatal collision occurred between two Conrail freight trains near Thompsonville, Pennsylvania. Four members of the crew were killed. Damages amounted to some $6 million. The National Transportation Safety Board, investigating the accident, found that the probable cause of the incident was "the sleep-deprived condition" of the crew.

In 1990, a crash on the Santa Fe railway killed four members of the crew and injured two others. Damages amounted to $4.4 million. The cause of the accident: The entire three-man crew on one train was sleeping.

On Friday, November 22, 1991, just before 7:30 A.M., two trains collided and derailed outside Eugene, Oregon. More than 8,000 gallons of diesel fuel was spilled. The diesel fuel subsequently ignited, causing significant traffic problems in the area. In property damage alone, the crash cost at least $3.3 million. Additional costs include those of the government's investigation; those associated with fighting the fire caused by the spilled diesel fuel; those involved in cleaning up the wreckage, the diesel fuel and the highway; those incurred by people who were adversely affected by the closed tracks and highway; and that incurred by Amtrak when it had to charter buses to take its passengers from the scene of the wreck into Portland. The engineer of the train at fault admitted that he had fallen asleep at the throttle.

A study of railroad engineers found that 11 percent fall asleep on most or all night shifts and 5 percent reported falling asleep on most or all early-morning shifts.

Military Operations: A Strategy for Sane Sleep Practices

Since many military operations take place at night, and all branches of the armed forces must be prepared for mobilization on a twenty-four-hour basis, sleep deprivation can become an important consideration in the services, too. Fit personnel have more endurance in the performance of physical tasks, even though physical fitness does not protect an individual from the effects of sleep deprivation.

Military operations involve many tasks that require constant vigilance, often under conditions that are not conducive to alertness. These include air defense radar and electronic surveillance personnel, sonar personnel, sentries, pickets, and so on. The performance of such tasks can degrade measurably after less than one hour on duty. Performance also is degraded by sleep loss and by being required to work at inappropriate times during the circadian cycle, regardless of the amount of rest.

When vigilance is required in sustained operations, naps can be effective, especially if taken during the predawn period from 2:00 to 6:00 A.M. However, relief from the task (i.e., simple rest) and sleep are the most effective means of regenerating one's vigilance.

Studies of the effects of fatigue on pilots indicate that physical coordination seems little degraded by drowsiness, even in extreme situations, but one's judgment degrades fairly quickly with the onset of fatigue. The military has guidelines for aircraft operations, but there are no crew guidelines for the operators of land or water vehicles.

For the first time, steps are being taken to assure that military commanders receive an adequate amount of sleep each night, and just recently, the biological clocks of some NASA astronauts were reset using high intensity light therapy to allow them to be awake and alert during a space shuttle launch and throughout the ensuing mission.

Road Hazards Ahead: Sleepy Truckers

Eight out of ten deaths in a heavy-truck accident are motorists who "just happened to be there."

Between 1982 and 1988, heavy-truck accidents caused 38,965 deaths in the United States. Most of the fatalities were *not* the truck drivers! Every commercial truck driver who dies on the highway takes an average of 4.2 innocent victims to the grave with him.

Of those killed in commercial trucking accidents each year, according to the National Highway Traffic Safety Administration, only 20 percent are the occupants of trucks; the other 80 percent are motorists, cyclists and pedestrians. An additional 30,000 people sustain injuries as the result of interstate trucking accidents.

The Association of Professional Sleep Societies says that motor vehicle accidents kill more than 50,000 people a year and that as many as 13 percent of them may be caused by drivers who fall asleep behind the wheel.

Almost one-third of the 182 truck drivers who were killed in highway accidents studied by the National Transportation Safety Board were judged to be fatigued. The study found that 10 percent of the drivers who were killed were under the influence of alcohol or drugs, but 31 percent were deemed "fatigued" based on studies of their driving logs and interviews with survivors and co-workers.

The National Transportation Safety Board now routinely reviews the work schedule of everyone involved in a trucking accident. It checks the seventy-two hours prior to the accident, and if the driver's schedule suggests sleep loss, the investigation may go back even further. Truck drivers face fines for driving without sleep. The Motor Carrier Act of 1935 allows a maximum of ten hours of driving before an extended rest — but the NTSB estimates that 58 to 91 percent of the nation's truckers ignore this law.

A case in point is the accident that occurred on July 14, 1986 near Brinkley, Arkansas. On that date, a truck collided with a bus, injuring the truck driver and twenty-seven passengers on the bus. It was later revealed that the truck driver had only a two-hour nap in the twenty-one hours prior to the crash. There was evidence that he had used both alcohol and marijuana, but the NTSB report following the accident said: "the combined effects of fatigue due to sleep deprivation, monotony, and the vulnerability to lapses of attention at that hour of the morning impaired the truck driver's vigilance and judgment and contributed to the crash."

When a roomful of truckers was asked by a researcher if they had fallen asleep behind the wheel, nearly all of them raised their hands.

All but a tiny fraction of truck drivers habitually get five hours sleep or less while they are on the road. A long-haul driver who covers up to 4,000 miles in seven to ten days often averages between two and four hours of sleep a night.

In a screening of 200 truck drivers at a major trucking company, nearly one-fourth of them were found to be troubled with sleep apnea. Many people believe that sleep apnea testing should be included in the medical examination required for commercial licenses.

At 7:00 A.M. on Monday, May 20, 1991, a tanker-truck carrying 8,800 gallons of gasoline near Montecito, California hit a guard rail, swerved, went out of control, overturned, and skidded down Highway 101. Driver Carroll Alestock told police he was driving at about 69 mph when he was jolted awake, then he kicked out the windshield and got out of the vehicle, unhurt, before it burst into flames. The spilled fuel caught fire, triggering several grass fires and endangering half a dozen homes. The accident halted northbound traffic on the busy highway for six and one-half hours, trapping thousands of commuters including former President Ronald Reagan, who had been en route to his ranch in Santa Ynez.

Truckers do not willingly take the blame for the result of their actions. They admit that 80 to 85 percent of the independent trucks violate the hours of service law and falsify their log books, but they claim that unreasonable delivery demands by their customers make it necessary to do so.

Since the deregulation of the trucking industry, far fewer of the nation's truckers are members of a union. Non-union drivers are more easily pressured by employers.

A Positive Model: Wal-Mart's Driver Safety Plan

Joe Michael, director of fleet safety for Wal-Mart Stores, Inc., feels differently. Wal-Mart has developed a driver safety plan that is a model for the industry. It is based upon a realistic view of the number of miles that a driver can cover safely in the course of a day. Michael says that under the Wal-Mart guidelines there aren't as many drivers arriving late, there are fewer accidents, the company suffers less loss due to truck maintenance, and their insurance premiums are lower. Wal-Mart has an accident rate of one in 1.3 million miles of travel compared to the national average of one in every 200,000 miles.

Lethal Public Transportation?

Beyond questions associated with sleep deprivation within the trucking industry, there are questions regarding those who drive buses, taxis and all other modes of public and private transportation. Merrill Mitler, a psychologist and sleep researcher at Scripps Clinic in La Jolla, California, sums up the situation when he says: "Many more people can be hurt when a train engineer or a nuclear technician falls asleep in 1990 than when a stagecoach driver fell asleep at the reins in 1890."

On June 27, 1990, en route to Buffalo, New York, the driver of a Greyhound bus fell asleep at the wheel. He had tried unsuccessfully to avoid dozing off by smoking a cigarette, drinking coffee, and listening to loud music, but eventually fell victim to his drowsiness. The driver and thirteen of his twenty-one passengers were injured.

In June 1991, another Greyhound driver dozed off at the wheel after making a stop in Pittsburgh and then traveling another sixty miles down the Pennsylvania Turnpike. He lost control of the vehicle, which went down a twenty-foot embankment, killing one woman and injuring fifteen others.

On August 3, 1991, the sleepy driver of a Greyhound bus went off the highway in New York and overturned. It was 6:15 a.m. One passenger was killed and over thirty others suffered broken bones, cuts and internal injuries. A sheriff's deputy concluded that the driver had fallen asleep at the wheel.

Is the Driver in the Next Lane Half Asleep?

Auto accidents in which the driver falls asleep tend to be more severe and often include a high-speed, head-on crash involving another auto or a stationary object of some sort. Of the accidents reported to the police each year, driver fatigue is cited as a factor in 72,000 cases or 1.1 percent of the total. Of those which result in a serious injury, 14,000 (2.9 percent) are caused, at least in part, by driver fatigue. Of those involving fatalities, 1,550 (3.4 percent) include drowsiness. A 1990 study by the National Transportation Safety Board of 182 fatal trucking accidents concluded that driver fatigue was the leading cause, at 31 percent.

Sleepiness seems to be the most likely cause of these accidents, says Dr. David Dinges, a biological psychologist at the University of Pennsylvania and one of the authors of the study. When measuring the alertness of airplane pilots and truck drivers, Dinges observed that the ability to sustain attention is reduced by at least 50 percent during normal sleep hours. If an entire night's sleep is lost, attention drops 70 percent. "If you go two nights without sleep," states Dinges, "you can barely function." Should sleep-deprived individuals have restrictions placed upon their licenses like those whose eyesight is impaired? Many believe that the licensing process should take sleep disorders into account.

The cost of car crashes totalled $137 billion in 1990 when loss of productivity and legal costs were factored in, according to Marion Blakey, administrator of the National Highway Traffic Safety Administration. Crashes in 1990 resulted in 44,500 deaths, 5.4 million injuries, and 28 million in vehicle damage.

Ford Motor Company is currently developing a tiny dashboard camera for use in automobiles. The camera records the rate at which drivers blink their eyes — which decreases as people become sleepy. Other sensors will collect information about how the driver is using the accelerator, brakes, and steering. When the camera and sensors detect that the driver is dangerously sleepy, a warning alarm will sound.

THE "SAFEST TEENAGE DRIVER IN AMERICA" BECAME A STATISTIC

Concord, New Hampshire

Seventeen-year-old Michael Doucette was the pride of his home town. He came from a nice family — three older brothers and a younger sister. He played first violin in the high school chamber orchestra and second violin in the New Hampshire Philharmonic. He even tutored other youngsters with an interest in the violin. Doucette was a member of the school chess and math clubs. He was on the school soccer and cross-country ski teams, and he played intramural lacrosse.

In May 1989, Doucette entered the New Hampshire Operation Driver Excellence Competition, won it, and took home $250 in cash and a $500 college scholarship. In July, he represented his home state in the national Dodge/AMVETS Operation Driver Excellence Competition in Detroit, and after two grueling days of tests, he won that, too, topping 51 contestants from other states and the District of Columbia.

Now officially "The Safest Teenage Driver in America," Doucette won a $5,000 college scholarship and the use of a new, red Dodge Shadow for one year. His high school received a second automobile in his name. Concord was proud of Michael, and Michael was proud of his victory. He drove the Dodge Shadow down Main Street in the city's annual New Year's Eve parade.

Two months later, Doucette and some friends

caravaned to Clarkson College in Potsdam, New York to see some friends and to look over the school. Afterward, they had lunch in Albany, New York then stopped in Keene, New Hampshire to visit some other friends. Less than 25 miles from home, Doucette fell asleep at the wheel, drifted across the yellow line, and hit a car coming the other way. Doucette, "The Safest Teenage Driver in America," was killed, along with the driver of the other car, a nineteen-year-old girl from nearby Lebanon. A passenger in the second car was hospitalized.

According to the driver of a car that was behind Doucette at the time of the accident, there was no indication of erratic driving until the car began to slow down without the brake lights having been applied. The witness reported that he might have seen Doucette's head bob just before the accident.

Shift Work and Sleep Deprivation

Shift workers and "moonlighters" have been shown to be far more accident-prone than traditional day workers. Yet 20 million people in America today, or one employed person out of five, is engaged in shift work — that is, they do not work a standard daytime schedule. Between 16 and 25 percent of our workforce works irregular hours. The most common around-the-clock schedule in use today causes a shift worker to change shifts every week, typically working fourteen out of fifteen consecutive days in the process.

In a typical compressed workweek, employees will work about forty hours in fewer than five days. This work may be performed ten to twelve hours per day, three or four days a week, with another three or four days off each week. Such twelve-hour shifts are common in the chemical industry, in the petroleum industry, on offshore oil rigs, in the ministeel industry, in the paper industry, in other manufacturing processes, in the utilities, in nursing and health care, in technical maintenance and computer operations, and even in clerical and administrative positions.

Often, shift work satisfies the workers because it allows them more days and weekends off.

One plant that uses the twelve-hour shift rotation reduced the number of days on the job from 273 per year to 182. With the twelve-hour rotating shift, fewer consecutive days are spent on the night shift and more time is allowed for recuperation between shifts than when eight-hour shifts are used five days a week. This may lessen the fatigue associated with rotating shifts and night work, but it also may encourage more moonlighting.

Using two twelve-hour shifts instead of three eight-hour shifts may be more cost-effective for the employer, and absenteeism seems to diminish when twelve-hour shifts are used. It is more difficult to replace an absent worker under those circumstances, however.

It also has been suggested that fewer errors and accidents occur on the twelve-hour shift and that productivity improves. Other studies, however, indicate that it may produce more fatigue, poorer sleep, and impaired psychomotor performance. Administrative problems also may arise because most laws and regulations have been based on the traditional eight-hour day, forty-hour week, so such things as the exposure limits to noise, chemicals and heat may have to be recalculated for the twelve-hour shift.

One study has indicated that 28 percent of the companies that go on a twelve-hour shift will return to the eight-hour, five-day shift. Older employees and women, especially those who have young children, seem to be less satisfied with the twelve-hour arrangement. The greatest number of shift workers are between thirty and forty-five years of age. Fifteen percent of the women in the workforce are shift workers.

A study by Richard M. Coleman, Clinical Assistant Professor in the Sleep Disorders Center at Stanford University's Medical School, has shown that 56 percent of the shift workers fall asleep at work on a regular basis. The worst offenders are those who work the night shift, when between 53 and 62 percent of the workers admit to regularly falling asleep on the job. During the day shift, between 27 and 35 percent do so; and on the evening shift, between 17 and 28 percent do so. Only eight to 18 percent of those who work on a straight daytime schedule fall asleep at work. A similar study done in Sweden reached the same conclusion.

Other researchers have found an alarming increase in the frequency of mishaps during the graveyard shift between 11:00 P.M. and 7:00 A.M. Between 4:00 and 6:00 A.M., for example, the rate of fatigue-related accidents involving trucks is ten times as high as the rate during the day.

Night workers and rotating shift workers also have three to five times more psychosocial problems, such as finding time for family obligations, performing community service, and other routine activities. The Office of Technology Assessment says marital problems and community alienation result from the strain placed on workers by such irregular schedules. According to a recent study by Nancy Anne Jenkins Hilliker and colleagues at the Deaconess Hospital Sleep Disorders Center in St. Louis, people who are "larks" or "morning types" may never adapt to their upside-down lifestyles, even after years on the job. Hilliker, once a night nursing supervisor, claims that three-quarters of the 6.8 million people who work night shifts in this country are sleepy every night and at least 20 percent actually fall asleep on the job, even when it may be dangerous for them or for the people under their care. Her study looked at the performances of two groups of self-described people — "night people" and "morning types" — who both got the same amount of sleep. Morning people performed demonstrably less well on a series of night-time tests.

In related research at the Sleep and Mood Disorders Laboratory at

Oregon Health Sciences University in Portland, Robert Stack looked at the relationship of the hormone melatonin to night-shift workers. Melatonin, which is secreted during nighttime sleep, is believed to reflect the state of the body clock, or circadian rhythms. Nighttime workers were found to be out of synchronization not only with day-active people but also with their own body clocks.

The average night worker sleeps less than the typical day worker. They're often up by noon because their brain and their bladder wake them up.

Sleep-deprived workers often tend to resort to alcohol or drugs to help them compensate for fatigue. The temptations to stop off at a bar with friends for an after-work drink — to "TGIF" on a Friday night — can make the situation a great deal worse. Studies show that it takes less alcohol to get a person drunk when he is tired.

Moonlighting Also Steals Sleep

An estimated 7.2 million Americans hold down two or more jobs, a figure that has increased 52 percent since 1980. This total includes 4.1 million men, most of them married; and 3.2 million women.

Of the men who hold down more than one job, 82.8 percent hold down one full-time job and one part-time job, 11.3 percent hold down two part-time jobs, and 5.8 percent work at two full-time jobs. On the average, men who hold two jobs work a total of 55.8 hours per week.

There has been a marked increase in the number of women working multiple jobs. Of all the people holding down two or more jobs today, 43 percent are women; in 1970, that figure was only 15 percent. Most of the women who work at more than one job are widowed, divorced or separated.

Of the women holding down more than one job, 64 percent work one full-time job and one part-time job, 33 percent work two part time jobs, and 2.9 percent work two full-time jobs. On the average, these multiple job-holders work an average of 47.1 hours per week.

Naturally, those who are working additional jobs are prone to do it at the sacrifice of an adequate amount of sleep.

According to the National Safety Council, accidents in the workplace cost the nation $63.8 billion in lost productivity, lost wages, property damage, insurance premiums, and medical expenses in 1990. If as little as one percent of that figure is sleep-related, that's an annual cost of $638 million attributable to sleep deprivation!

Among shift workers, absenteeism also runs much higher than it does among those who work a straight daytime schedule.

Furthermore, an employer who allows an employee to work too many hours without rest may be found negligent in cases where the employee later causes an accident, even after the employee has already left the job site.

All employers who require shift work would be well advised to:

1. Discuss lifestyle changes which may be caused by changes in employees' work schedules.

2. Monitor problems observed.

3. Be willing to change shift assignments if sleep or other health problems develop.

Sleep Deprivation in the Medical Profession

As strange as it may seem, the members of the medical profession seem to be among the least informed about the dangers of sleep deprivation — and among the worst offenders.

Health care is a twenty-four-hour-a-day business; there can be no argument about that. Yet the staffing of our medical institutions actually tends to *create* sleep-restricting situations that are totally out of keeping with sound judgment. A resident on call at night, for example, is often responsible for the care of forty to sixty patients. In some inner-city hospitals, first-year residents may have as many as fifteen new admissions a night. Yet some residents work more than 130 hours a week in shifts of twelve to sixty hours' duration, with every other night on call!

THE IMPACT OF SLEEP-DEPRIVED HEALTH CARE WORKERS: THE CASE OF LIBBY ZION

New York, New York

Libby Zion was admitted to New York Hospital-Cornell University Medical Center through the emergency room in 1984.

She died a few hours later.

Ms. Zion's father, a prominently-connected individual in New York, sued the hospital. It was discovered that although eight hours had elapsed from the time Ms. Zion entered the emergency room to the time she died, she was not examined by an emergency room attending physician. Instead, she had been treated by an intern and a junior resident, both of whom had been on duty for *eighteen* hours prior to her admission.

The New York grand jury failed to hand down any indictments in the case, but it did find:

Lack of sleep degrades care given by medical staff. That the number of hours that interns and residents are required to work is not conducive to providing quality medical care.

Unsupervised medical trainees can endanger patients. That major medical decisions were being made by inexperienced physicians, acting alone and unsupervised, which can result in mistakes, sometimes with fatal consequences.

Mistakes by inexperienced medical personnel may be related to lack of sleep. That the likelihood that such mistakes can occur is increased by the long hours that interns and residents are forced to work.

The grand jury severely criticized the New York graduate medical education system and made several strong recommendations on how to improve it. Among them was the proposal that the State Department of Health establish regulations that would limit the number of consecutive hours that interns and junior residents can work.

Under pressure, the New York Commissioner of Health proposed new rules, under which there would be a twelve-hour limit on emergency room shifts for both house staff and attending physicians. The scheduled workweek for other house staff in designated acute care specialties should not exceed an average of eighty hours over a four-week period. No scheduled shift should exceed twenty-four consecutive hours. On-duty assignments should be separated by at least eight hours, with one twenty-four-hour period off work each week.

The cost of implementing these new policies was estimated by the State of New York at $226 million, which increased its budget by three percent. In addition, they estimated that the changes would cost a total of $3.1 billion over the next ten years, and $5.7 billion over the next fifteen years.

Unfortunately, the new rules are said to be widely ignored. The regulations are worded in such a way as to require that no resident should be *scheduled* to work more than twelve hours in the emergency room or for more than eighty hours *average* over a four-week period.

Interestingly, no other state has followed suit, although the teaching hospitals in Massachusetts have undertaken a voluntary effort to change the working conditions of residents. In all, only slightly more than half of the hospitals in the Council of Teaching Hospitals had policies regarding residents' hours as of 1991. Of those, Veterans Administration hospitals and church-affiliated hospitals were above the average, while other non-profit hospitals, municipal hospitals, and state hospitals all fell short of the average.

Prior to the implementation of the new regulations cited above, it was reported that first-year residents in New York averaged only a little over two and a half hours of sleep per day!

Creating a simple rotation by which interns and residents were allowed to take short naps during their duty hours would alleviate many of the potential hazards of the present system, yet in many programs an intern who is caught sleeping during his shift is severely reprimanded.

Nurses Are Sleep-Deprived Also

Nurses often are scheduled for shifts that are almost as unrealistic as those worked by some interns and residents.

A nurse in a West Coast hospital had been working all night and was in the twelfth hour of a twelve-hour shift. She also was under pressure to complete her work assignments before her shift ended. While disconnecting a patient's IV, she was accidentally stuck by the needle, which turned out to be contaminated with HIV-infected blood. The nurse seroconverted and is now HIV-positive.

A malpractice suit was filed against a nurse in the Northeast because a patient had died under her care while she was working her second consecutive eight-hour shift. In another Northeastern hospital, a nurse had been put on restricted duty due to a heart condition. Nonetheless, she was scheduled to work an eighteen-hour shift. Since she was on medication, she increased the dosage to help cover the demands of the long work hours. When she then became ill, she — along with fourteen other nurses —submitted her case to labor arbitration.

Some nurses have a means of redress because they are represented by a union. Even if they believe that shift work is causing problems, they may find it hard to do much about it, however, unless the issue of shift work has been previously covered in their collective bargaining agreements.

Such unions as the American Nurses Association; Service Employees International Union; American Federation of State, County and Municipal Employees; and Federation of Nurses and Health Professionals, a division of the American Federation of Teachers, will use shift work as a "bargaining chip" when they are negotiating new contracts. Often in contention are such questions as:

> Length of shifts
>
> Length of time between shifts
>
> Split shifts
>
> Shift of choice

Non-union nurses often work at facilities that have no formal grievance procedures, so they have even less recourse in such situations.

Teach the Teachers: Physician Training Must Change

To a considerable extent, the problem in the medical profession stems from the fact that very few doctors and nurses have received any training in sleeping disorders and sleep deprivation themselves! If they knew more about sleep deprivation, what causes it and what the consequences can be, they would be in a much better position not only to fight against the injustices in their own field, but to educate their patients on the benefits of developing better sleeping habits.

According to a Gallup poll conducted in 1991, physicians failed to diagnose or even identify the one in three adults who suffer from insomnia. Why is that significant? Here are some reasons:

> Waking earlier than desired in the morning is one of the most common symptoms of ordinary depression.
>
> Insomnia and sleep disruption are common features of the psychoses, including schizophrenia, which alone affects over

two million Americans over the course of their lifetimes and represents 40 percent of all hospitalized psychiatric patients in the U.S.

Disturbed sleep is a prominent feature of manic-depressive illness, which affects one million Americans.

The disgraceful fact is that American medical schools today teach only 20 minutes worth of material related to sleep during an entire four-year course of study!

When the family physician does not recognize or lightly dismisses a sleep problem, the patient is not likely to know enough about the subject to press the matter. Policy-makers, regulators, and industry all too often cast a blind eye to the potential effects of sleep deprivation in the workplace, in commerce, in war, and in peace.

In the nation's medical schools, four percent of the programs in neurology, nine percent of those in psychiatry, 12 percent of those in family practice, and 18 percent of those in pediatrics offer *no* instruction of any kind on sleep and sleep disorders! Only 19 percent of the internships and 34 percent of the doctoral programs offer formal class-room training in sleep and sleep disorders.

There are 2.5 million registered nurses in the United States, but when the undergraduate training programs for nurses were sampled, it was learned that 63 percent of them presented one hour or less of content regarding normal sleep, nearly 56 percent offered one hour or less of content regarding sleep disruptions and problems, and nearly 76 percent provided one hour or less of content on primary sleep disorders.

With fewer than ten exceptions among America's approximately 2,000 colleges and universities, no systematic teaching about sleep and sleep disorders exists. Moreover, when approximately fifty standard textbooks of introductory psychology and biology were examined, none was found to contain useful information about sleep deprivation and sleep disorders.

Sleep disorders are not discussed at length, if at all, in medical schools, physician residency programs, nursing programs, or education afforded other healthcare professionals today!

For some people, the results are catastrophic.

What Can *You* Do?

If You Drink, Don't Drive — *Especially* if You Are Tired. Fatigue is a factor in many accidents that are blamed on alcohol. Prior sleep loss greatly enhances the sedating or sleep-inducing effects of alcohol, and a substantial portion of the population (perhaps 25 percent or more) are so chronically sleep-deprived that one beer could make them drunk. Some 22,000 Americans died in alcohol-related crashes in 1990.

TGIF, but Take Care. Driving home on a Friday is a greater risk than on a Monday, when you haven't been deprived of sleep all week.

Watch Out for Medications. Even widely-used cold and hayfever remedies can be dangerous when used while driving. Benadryl®, an over-the-counter antihistamine, contains the same drug that is used in the sleep preparation Nytol®, for example. Newer second generation antihistamines such as Seldane® are not sleep-inducing and may be better suited for use by people who plan to drive a car.

Teach Your Children. Sleep-impaired novice drivers (most often teenagers) are at extremely high risk. They are the highest risk group for fatal auto injuries — yet Drivers Education classes in the schools do not include driver fatigue as a factor in driving safety. Talk with your teenagers about the relationship between fatigue and driving performance, and when they are overtired, take the keys away.

Take Sensible Precautions. Allow for adequate rest stops when planning trips. Don't start a car trip in the evening or when you are overtired from last-minute preparations or finishing up at work. When you feel yourself becoming sleepy while driving, pull over and nap briefly.

Support Reasonable Actions. If you are the decision-maker in your work environment, heed the facts of human sleep need when making schedules and setting goals. If you are not the decision-maker, it may be possible for you to bring the facts to the attention of one who is. Support the efforts of community workers such as fire marshals and police chiefs who are attempting to respond wisely to the real issues concerning sleep and human performance.

CHAPTER FOUR

Primary Sleep Disorders

**S**ome people sleep too little, or too fitfully. Others seem to sleep too much — or to fall asleep at inopportune times. In serious sleep disorders, these are the *symptoms* of serious sleep-related problems. The "trick" is to find the root cause of the disorder. When it is cured, the symptoms will go away.

In order to do that, of course, it is important to determine just what form of sleep disorder is at the root of the problem. This calls for consulting a physician — and sometimes even a specialist who has received special training in handling sleep disorders.

If *all* sleep disorders sprang from the same source, treatment would be simpler. Unfortunately, that is not the case. There are several conditions that can produce a sleeping disorder.

Sleep Apnea

Sleep apnea is a condition that was discovered only recently (in 1965, in Europe). Between 70 and 90 percent of those who suffer from it are men, mostly middle-aged, and usually overweight. The vast majority snore heavily. The problem is a neuromuscular one that results in the partial closing of an airway called the nasal pharynx while one sleeps. *Apnea* is a word of Greek origin that literally means "without breath." Up to 10 percent of the male population, up to five percent of all adult women, and up to 40 percent of all Americans over the age of sixty may suffer from some form of sleep apnea. There is some evidence that sleep apnea is caused by a defect in the central nervous system.

Sleep Apnea and Snoring

Scientists estimate that 30 million Americans snore — and that 2.5 million of them suffer from sleep apnea. Who has not encountered someone at some time who snores? It is a universal nuisance, a condition as common as the cold — and the sources of countless confrontations between husbands and wives since time began. Snoring is caused by impaired breathing as we sleep, and the older we get the more likely we are to snore. Over all, one of every eight Americans snores. And it is estimated that almost 60 percent of the men and 45 percent of the women who have reached their sixties snore.

Light snoring may be a minor nuisance, but when snoring becomes loud and disruptive, and when it is accompanied by extreme sleepiness or sleep attacks during the daytime, it should be taken seriously. It could be a sign of sleep apnea, a life-threatening condition that results from the blockage of one's breathing during sleep.

Who Is At Risk?

Young blacks are at greater risk than young whites. There also is a definite link between obesity and sleep apnea in both black and Hispanic women. Since obesity is a much greater problem in poor females, particularly black females, sleep apnea may be more prevalent in black families.

Apnea is less common in pre-menopausal women than it is in men. Differences in the anatomy and female hormones appear to protect women from the illness until the onset of menopause.

The ailment is particularly frequent and particularly severe among the patients confined to nursing homes. In one nursing home studied, more than one-third of the patients were found to have sleep apnea syndrome but none was being treated for this problem.

Risk factors other than age include cranio-facial abnormalities; endocrine dysfunction, such as thyroid deficiencies or excess growth hormone; and genetic factors. Particularly susceptible to the ailment are people who have a deviated nasal septum (often incurred by a blow to the nose while participating in sports), polyps, enlarged tonsils, or large adenoids.

Alcohol, tobacco and drug use also aggravate the condition.

Symptoms of Sleep Apnea

Those who suffer from sleep apnea actually *stop breathing* as they sleep — perhaps as often as several hundred times per night. Psychologist Thomas Roth, chief of the sleep disorder center at Detroit's Henry Ford Hospital, says: "A person with apnea might not even be aware that he woke up 500 to 1,000 times during the night."

Patients seem to gasp for breath in their sleep, and the oxygen level in their blood becomes abnormally low. In severe cases, the patient may actually spend more time *not breathing* than breathing!

Those who suffer from sleep apnea do a lot of loud and intermittent snoring during the night. They may have the sensation of choking, and may move about a great deal while in bed. Excessive sweating often occurs during sleep. There often is an irregular pounding of the heart as the patient gasps for breath.

People who have sleep apnea may suffer from early-morning headaches and feel excessively sleepy throughout the day. Hallucinations sometimes occur while the patient is awake but feeling extremely sleepy. Memory deterioration, personality changes, and impotence are common. Rapid weight gains, often approaching obesity, often occur.

When apnea occurs in children, it commonly causes bedwetting, and such episodes may occur more than once a night. Bedwetting side effects also have been known to occur in adult sufferers of the illness.

Sufferers are hard to awaken, and if they are suddenly awakened, they frequently do not know where they are. Upon awaking, those who suffer from "the snoring sickness" usually will not recall having experienced an apneic episode in their sleep. A period of disorientation sometimes occurs immediately after waking. During such periods, the individual may have difficulty with his memory and give inappropriate answers to questions, acting as if he did not hear it or failed to understand what was asked.

The excessive daytime sleepiness caused by sleep apnea may lead to problems at work, problems with the family, and problems dealing with friends. It often causes irritability, decreased productivity or injuries on the job, motor vehicle accidents, and disrupted and disruptive family and social relationships.

In its most severe form, sleep apnea may produce fatal pulmonary and cardiovascular complications. Cardiovascular problems resulting from the illness may include high blood pressure, irregular heart rhythm, or deterioration of the heart muscle and its ability to pump blood, which can result in heart failure, heart attack or stroke.

Apnea patients have twice the usual prevalence of hypertension, three times as much heart disease, and four times as much cerebrovascular disease. Other potential consequences include stroke, neuropsychiatric problems, cognitive impairment, sexual dysfunction, and injury due to accidents. Once a person develops sleep apnea, he appears to have it for life.

At least a million people are severely impaired by the ailment, and twice that many are partially impaired. Unfortunately, 95 percent of them remain undiagnosed and untreated.

Seriousness of the Condition

Those who suspect that they may suffer from sleep apnea should be aware that it is potentially a life-threatening condition requiring prompt medical attention. Drugs that depress the central nervous system, which controls breathing, could lead to the patient's death. Therefore the use of alcohol, sleeping pills, tranquilizers, and barbiturates is very dangerous for apnea sufferers.

During an apneic episode, there are serious abnormalities of the heart and blood vessels. The oxygen content of the blood decreases and the carbon dioxide level increases, meaning that the heart, brain and other vital tissues are periodically deprived of needed oxygenated blood. The blood pressure rises sharply in both the pulmonary and systemic arteries. The heart slows (bradycardia) and may stop entirely (asystole) for as long as six to eight seconds.

The elevated blood pressure that a patient experiences in his sleep during an apneic episode may eventually remain elevated during the daytime when the patient's breathing is normal, thereby providing a possible reason for otherwise unexplained hypertension.

Severe sleep apnea can cause death from cardiac arrhythmias that occur during a nighttime attack.

More than 38,000 cardiovascular deaths a year may be due to sleep apnea. Patients with sleep apnea have seven times as many auto accidents as those who do not have apnea, and 24 percent of them report having fallen asleep at the wheel — at least once a week!

Sleep apnea has been implicated in some cases of Sudden Infant Death Syndrome (sometimes called SIDS or crib death).

THE TOLL OF SLEEP APNEA: THE JERRY GILL CASE

Wayne, Pennsylvania

Jerry Gill's case of sleep apnea was first diagnosed in November 1984 during a visit to the Sleep Clinic at the Medical College of Pennsylvania. The following year, Gill underwent surgery to alleviate his problem, and the doctor prescribed the drug Dilantin® for short-term post-operative treatment.

In 1988, Gill suffered a severe nocturnal seizure. The doctor resumed his Dilantin treatments and recommended another visit to the Sleep Clinic, where it was determined that his condition had worsened over the three intervening years. In June, Gill's seizures resumed.

Gill developed a fear of driving, particularly at night, and of losing his driver's license. He developed a fear of spending the night away from home alone. He began to fear that he would become uninsurable. As a result, he felt that he had to maintain the coverage offered by his employer's carrier, which reduced his job mobility.

Gill's wife Sheryl began to experience sleepless nights as she forced herself to keep one ear open, listening to her husband's breathing so that she could awaken him when it became irregular.

Jerry grew apathetic. His lack of motivation kept him from completing jobs or following through on details. He resisted facing family issues when they appeared. His short-term memory showed signs of deteriorating, and he grew fearful of falling asleep and not waking up.

Gill's three sons became concerned that their father's condition might be hereditary.

Then, during the night of December 14, 1988, Jerry Gill died. His autopsy report was marked "Unexplained Sudden Death."

How Sleep Apnea is Diagnosed

Patients undergoing polysomnography are admitted to a sleep disorders center.

On the night of the study, they go to the sleep laboratory about an hour before their usual bedtime. There, technicians position dime-sized sensors at various spots on their body to record brain waves, muscle activity, leg and arm movements, heart rhythms, and other body functions while they sleep.

Several devices are used to assess different aspects of breathing. Either a light mask is placed over the nose and mouth or temperature-sensitive beads are taped at these sites to measure the rate at which air enters and leaves the body. Stretch bands with small gauges are worn around the chest and abdomen to show the effort needed to breathe. A device is clipped onto the earlobe to chart the decline in the level of oxygen during each apnea.

The patient's sleep also may be studied during the day, and a series of naps may be offered at two-hour intervals as a means of documenting daytime sleepiness (the Multiple Sleep Latency Test).

Other possible examinations include various x-rays and the direct examination of the air passage with fiber optics.

Even with competent medical supervision, sleep apnea cannot be reliably diagnosed *except* when the patient's oxygen intake and other telltale conditions are monitored *while he is sleeping.* Medical examination of a person suffering from sleep apnea will reveal absolutely no characteristic physical abnormalities while the person is awake, but if the sounds of breathing are closely observed as the patient sleeps, a characteristic cycle of heavy snoring, followed by silence, followed by more heavy snoring can be heard. Only a specialized test known as polysomnography can provide a definitive analysis of the patient's condition.

Sleep Apnea Can Be Successfully Treated

Highly successful clinical treatments have been available for sleep apnea for years, but most primary care physicians are not aware of them.

The drug Vivactil® (protriptyline) seems to benefit those with relatively mild obstructive sleep apnea. It also diminishes the level of snoring. Unfortunately, it produces a number of unpleasant side effects such as "dry mouth," constipation, and urinary retention.

Sometimes, the problem can be cured simply by having the patient lose weight. Sometimes, simply sleeping on one's side can affect a cure.

Mouth devices that help keep the airway open during the night are designed to bring the jaw forward, elevate the soft palate, or retain the tongue.

Some people have a smaller jaw or a smaller throat opening at the back of the throat. Some have a large tongue, enlarged tonsils, or other tissues that partially block the entrance to the airway. Removing the tonsils and adenoids (more common in children than in adults), nasal polyps, or other growths sometimes alleviates the symptoms.

In particularly severe cases, other types of surgery may be required. A procedure called uvulo-palato-pharyngoplasty (UPP) involves surgically removing excess tissue at the back of the throat to enable a better flow of air. UPP seems to benefit about half of those who undergo the procedure, although a few of the patients report troublesome post-operative effects such as nasal speech or the regurgitation of liquids into the nose when swallowing.

Over the last decade, surgical procedures also have been developed to reposition the jaw in order to make the airway passage larger.

Sometimes, a tracheostomy is performed. In this procedure, a small hole is created in the neck below and in front of the Adam's apple. A small tube is inserted in this hole, and at night a valve in this tube is opened, allowing air to bypass the patient's upper passageway. During the day, the valve is closed, enabling the patient to breathe and speak normally.

In more severe situations, a technique called Continuous Positive Air Pressure (CPAP) may be employed. With this treatment, a machine blows air into the patient's nose throughout the night, keeping the air passages in the throat open. Unlike a respirator, which does the patient's breathing for him, the CPAP equipment provides air in a constant and regulated manner so that there is just enough pressure to hold the patient's throat open when it tends to relax the most.

Unfortunately, many patients stop using the CPAP equipment

because it is uncomfortable — something like sleeping with a vacuum in your ears and a scuba mask on your face.

A similar device, called BiPap, uses different pressures when the patient inhales or exhales, but its use is much more selective.

More recently, a new treatment that electrically stimulates the upper airway muscles during sleep has been developed in Japan. The technique is currently being studied in the United States.

Narcolepsy

Narcolepsy is a neurological disorder, possibly resulting from a biochemical defect that affects the neurotransmitters in the central nervous system. It generally manifests itself first during an individual's teenage years, but it can occur at any age. It is rare, however, for narcolepsy to first appear in someone who is past forty. Narcolepsy afflicts both sexes equally and tends to run through families.

Sufferers tend to get poor grades in school and to have numerous study problems due to their inability to read, study, concentrate, memorize, or pay attention. Later in life, this places limitations on their career alternatives, resulting in a low level of job satisfaction, frequent job loss, a loss of income, and low self-esteem.

Narcoleptics frequently suffer from poor interpersonal relationships. They tend to become alcoholics, have high divorce rates, suffer from a decreased sexual libido and impotence, and experience a great deal of depression and other psychiatric problems.

Here is how one witness expressed her feelings of deprivation at a National Commission on Sleep Disorders hearing:

> I have lived with the symptoms of narcolepsy for at
> least forty-five years. My father, employed by the
> Federal government as Regional Director of the
> Department of Labor, spent thousands and thou-
> sands of government insurance dollars paid to many

physicians over a period of twenty years in an effort to find out what was wrong with his little girl. During those twenty years I unknowingly lived with a disabling, hidden handicap. Despite a high IQ, I dropped out of college. Prior to diagnosis, I was directly responsible for several near-fatal automobile accidents. I received a diagnosis only because of a three-paragraph article in the *San Francisco Chronicle*.

The simple joys and pleasures everyone takes for granted — to work and achieve, to sit and read a good book by the fire, to engage in a stimulating conversation at the table after dinner, to enjoy the symphony or a play or the opera, to attend church and worship on Sunday mornings — the quality of all these things would, for the most part, be denied me. I would literally sleep the rest of my life away.

Incidence of the Disease

Once thought to be a rather rare disease, scientists now realize that narcolepsy is as prevalent as multiple sclerosis, Parkinson's disease or hemophilia. Comedian Lenny Bruce had it. Los Angeles Dodgers' team physician Dr. Frank Jobe has it. Computer software pioneer, entrepreneur, and philanthropist Joseph A. Piscopo has it.

The American Narcolepsy Association estimates that approximately one person in every 1,000 may be affected by narcolepsy. Other estimates vary from one-quarter to half a million, but all knowledgeable agencies admit that a very small percentage of those who have the ailment have been properly diagnosed and treated.

Diagnosis of Narcolepsy

Since the symptoms of the disorder often begin mildly and build up slowly over the years, those who suffer from it usually don't seek help for their ailment for as many as five to seven years.

Typically, it takes examinations by about five different doctors and the passing of nearly fifteen years before a narcoleptic is properly diagnosed and can begin to receive treatment.

How Can Narcolepsy Be Spotted?

Because of narcolepsy's telltale symptoms and the age at which they generally begin to appear, teachers would seem to be the most likely ones to spot the ailment in its early stages — if they were trained to look for it. Unfortunately, sleep disorders are not a part of the health curriculum to which teachers are exposed, which helps to explain why only 20 to 50 percent of the nation's narcoleptics have been properly diagnosed.

A mother poignantly described her frustrations about her son's situation at school to the National Commission on Sleep Disorders hearing:

> My son has narcolepsy. He has been branded by the local education system as lazy, day dreaming, incompetent, argumentative, lacking imagination and motivation. They recommend psychiatric counseling and placement in behavioral disorder classes . . . it's sad that we're doing this to a lot of kids. My boy is a bright, good looking teenager of sixteen. He has a good sense of humor and is extremely talented, creative, and inventive. He has a lot to offer. I am begging and pleading that someone intervene on behalf of my son and others. It's time the medical and educational system woke up to the fact that this is a medical disorder. The ridicule, humiliation, and labeling must be stopped and replaced by knowledge and research, possible cures and adequate treatment.

The Symptoms of Narcolepsy

Those who suffer from narcolepsy complain of excessive daytime sleepiness, often expressed as tiredness, lack of energy or irresistible sleepiness. Sometimes, outsiders falsely attribute these symptoms to laziness, malingering or a psychiatric disorder.

Those who suffer from the ailment may suddenly drop off to sleep — at any time. Most commonly, attacks occur while the individual is watching TV, reading, listening to a lecture or engaging in an activity that does not have his or her full attention, but one also can occur while the person is walking, riding a bicycle, eating, engaging in a conversation, or even driving a car. Attacks can occur without regard to the quality or quantity of sleep that the individual received the night before.

This is how a narcolepsy patient described his life on an average day.

> To help you understand narcolepsy, set your alarm for every ninety minutes, and stay awake for ten minutes each time it goes off. Alternate that with periods of forty-eight hours without sleep. Collapse on the floor each time you are angry, scared, surprised, laughing or upset. Sleep for half an hour before you drive anywhere; sleep again for half an hour when you arrive. Be late for everything. Fall asleep at every traffic light. I figured out the difference between my life as a narcoleptic and dead people. The dead don't have to get up and go to work every day.

Nearly half of the known narcoleptics report having fallen asleep at the wheel of their automobiles at least once. One-fourth of them report having had accidents caused by falling asleep at the wheel.

Many sufferers are men and women who are unable to work outside the home due to their constant sleepiness or to achieve a normal quality of life due to the effects of their illness. Many are unable to obtain adequate life, health and disability insurance without costly exclusions, limitations and premium surcharges. Many have been unable to obtain reimbursement for treatment under medicare and medicaid. Many have been denied disability claims under Social Security programs.

Some narcoleptics have lost their driving privileges or had severe restrictions put upon them. In Maryland, for example, persons under treatment for narcolepsy may not be considered for any class of license until they have been free of symptoms for at least one year and are experiencing no side effects from medications.

THE CASE OF DR. FRANK JOBE

Los Angeles, California

Dr. Frank Jobe, the Dodgers' orthopedic surgeon, is one of the most important, visible members of the organization. Yet to the players, he is known simply as the eyes behind the mask.

Behind the mask there is the face of a renowned orthopedic surgeon who returned to the news after performing landmark shoulder reconstruction that returned Orel Hershiser to the mound for the first-place Dodgers.

Jobe has ministered to other injured sports stars such as Tommy John, George Brett, Jerry West, Wilt Chamberlain, Jim McMahon, Jerry Pate, Paul Azinger and Ivan Lendl. But he sometimes can't stay awake during staff meetings, and used to employ a driver because of a tendency to doze behind the wheel.

Several years ago it was discovered that Jobe has narcolepsy. It never affects him during surgery, but he has fallen asleep during everything from lectures to sales pitches.

"It happened once when these sales representatives were at the research lab, showing us this important equipment," Jobe recalled with a chuckle. "Right in the middle of their big spiel, they looked down to see that the guy they were trying to sell (me) was sitting in the front row, fast asleep."

Jobe needs no medication, and has since discharged his driver. But he can't rid his family of their worries.

"Sure we worry, because you can die from this," said his son Christopher. "We all really worry about him driving home at night. We're fortunate Dodger Stadium is a pretty easy drive to his house late at night."

On occasion, narcoleptics may experience a sudden weakness in their muscles — a condition called cataplexy. The effects of this condition may range from a partial weakness in the muscles that lasts for only a few seconds to a complete loss of muscle control that lasts for a full minute or two. In severe situations, the sufferer may be close to total physical collapse, unable to move or even to speak, but still conscious and at least partially aware of activities going on in the immediate area.

An attack of cataplexy is always — and only — triggered by some emotional reaction, such as laughter, elation, anger, or surprise. It may range from a sudden jerking of the head to a complete physical collapse, causing the individual to fall to the ground. Attacks may last for a brief moment or last for several minutes.

Even though narcoleptics do not experience the loss of bladder and bowel control or the tongue-biting that characterize epilepsy, narcoleptics have occasionally been misdiagnosed as epileptics when one of their attacks of cataplexy is mistakenly believed to be an epileptic seizure. Narcolepsy is not similar, or in any way related, to epilepsy.

Narcoleptics may experience bizarre and vivid dreams while they are falling asleep or awaking. Such hypnagogic hallucinations are vivid, realistic and sometimes frightening auditory or visual perceptions. As a result, some patients have been incorrectly diagnosed as schizophrenic.

Indeed, well-intended but untrained or poorly-informed physicians have misdiagnosed narcolepsy as depression, hypothyroidism, and even encephalitis. To the public, they have been categorized as lazy, rebellious, and disinterested, or even as dangerous, psychotic or drug users. A witness testifying at a sleep disorders hearing in Washington, DC. related that after years of suffering, he was diagnosed at age forty-five as having a brain tumor. Brain surgery was scheduled but, during a routine spinal tap, the narcoplepsy victim had cataplexy. An attending resident saved him from brain surgery when she diagnosed his condition — at last correctly — as narcolepsy.

At night, narcoleptics tend to doze off immediately but they often experience disturbed nighttime sleeping, including tossing and turning in bed, leg jerks, nightmares, and frequent awakenings. They may experience a momentary inability to move called "sleep paralysis" when falling asleep or awakening. They may demonstrate "automatic behavior" — the performance of a task with no later recollection of having done it. Often, narcoleptics experience visual problems, especially difficulty in focusing, drooping eyelids, double vision, flickering sensations, and a sensitivity to light.

Narcolepsy affects the individual's ability to study, concentrate, read, and listen attentively. With its typical onset in the early teenage years, these effects can be the cause of failures in school for many adolescents.

Treating Narcolepsy

Some researchers think that narcolepsy may be caused by a genetic defect, and although there is no known cure for the disorder, it often can be brought under control through the use of stimulant drugs.

A definitive diagnosis of the condition may require a polysomnogram, which requires that the patient be drug-free for at least fifteen days prior to the test (a very difficult requirement for those who need drugs in order to sustain anything approximating a "normal" lifestyle). It also requires that the patient enter a clinic or a hospital for one overnight and one all-day visit. The total cost may run from $1,600 to $2,400, some or all of which may not be covered by insurance.

Pupillography is a candidate for further research in the study of narcolepsy. A pupillometer is an electronic instrument which measures the diameter of a subject's pupils with two infra-red television cameras. A narcoleptic's pupils distinctly identify atypical patterns of oscillations and shrinking diameters in less than fifteen minutes of testing in a darkened room. The procedure might have the potential to become an inexpensive screening tool for narcolepsy in the future.

Another avenue of research came from Japan in 1984 when a study showed that narcoleptics there tested positively for a Human Leukocyte Antigen (HLA) known as DRw15. As a screening process, this test could be performed at less than half the cost of undertaking a polysomnogram.

Excessive daytime sleepiness usually is treated with stimulant drugs; the cataplexy and other REM-sleep symptoms with antidepressant drugs. This need for a constant supply of drugs can cause many problems for a narcoleptic due to inconsistent government drug regulations, the scrutiny of federal Drug Enforcement Administration agents, and difficulties in dealing with various state drug control agencies.

Since amphetamine addicts have been known to fake the symptoms of narcolepsy in order to gain easy, legal access to the drugs, sufferers of the ailment commonly get harassed by drug control agents.

In some states, there is a specific time limit within which a prescription must be filled or it becomes void. Others prohibit mailed prescriptions or mail-order pharmacy services. Still others require a visit to the doctor every time a new prescription is required.

Other states place a restriction on specific drugs or on the dosage levels that may be prescribed by a physician. Some limit prescriptions to no more than a thirty-day supply of the medication. The federal and state regulations impose a considerable and often unwarranted burden and cost upon the patient, the physician and the pharmacist.

Physicians who are willing to prescribe these medications often prefer to use substances that are not subject to as much government control or to prescribe lower dosages of the controlled substances, which thereby increases the number of under-medicated patients. The federal and state regulations also adversely affect the cost and availability of these medications, which are vital to narcoleptics who wish to live reasonably normal lives.

It is important for narcoleptics to establish a regular bedtime and for them to get an uninterrupted night's sleep every night. Short naps during the day also may help. They should avoid situations at work and at leisure that may put them or those around them in danger.

Estimates made in 1990 placed the cost of narcolepsy to the nation at a minimum of $64.1 million.

✍ Do You Have a Sleep Disorder?

Ask yourself these questions:

❑ yes ❑ no Do you snore loudly each night?

❑ yes ❑ no Do you have frequent pauses in breathing while you sleep (you stop breathing for ten seconds or longer)?

❑ yes ❑ no Are you restless during sleep, tossing and turning from one side to another?

❏ yes ❏ no Does your posture during sleep seem unusual?

❏ yes ❏ no Do you wake up frequently and without a reason?

❏ yes ❏ no Do you have to get up to urinate several times during the night?

❏ yes ❏ no Have you wet your bed?

❏ yes ❏ no Have you fallen from bed?

❏ yes ❏ no Do you wake up in the morning tired and foggy, not ready to face the day?

❏ yes ❏ no Do you have headaches in the morning?

❏ yes ❏ no Are you very sleepy during the day?

❏ yes ❏ no Do you have difficulty concentrating, being productive, and completing tasks at work?

❏ yes ❏ no Do you carry out routine tasks in a daze?

❏ yes ❏ no Have you ever arrived home in your car but couldn't remember the trip from work?

❏ yes ❏ no Are you having serious relationship problems at home, with friends and relatives, or at work?

❏ yes ❏ no Are you afraid that you may be out of touch with the real world, unable to think clearly, losing your memory, or emotionally ill?

❏ yes ❏ no Do your friends tell you that you're not like yourself?

❏ yes ❏ no Are you depressed?

❏ yes ❏ no Are you irritable and angry, especially first thing in the morning?

❑ yes ❑ no Are you overweight?

❑ yes ❑ no Do you have high blood pressure?

❑ yes ❑ no Do you have pains in your bones and joints?

❑ yes ❑ no Do you have trouble breathing through your nose?

❑ yes ❑ no Do you often have a drink of alcohol before going to
            bed?

❑ yes ❑ no If you are a man, is your collar size seventeen inches or
            larger?

Answering Yes to any of these questions may be a clue that an underlying problem exists. That problem may be sleep apnea, another sleep disorder, or a problem not related to sleep. Each of these questions points to a symptom. They are the clues, sometimes subtle and perceived only by the patient (such as memory loss), and sometimes overt and observable by friend or family (such as snoring) that indicate that the mind or body is diseased. Your doctor, trained to see symptoms as the manifestation of disease, can help you interpret and understand the basis of your condition.

CHAPTER FIVE

Other Sleep Problems

I n all, sleep researchers have identified nearly 100 different sleep disorders. The ones described in the previous chapter are the most common or the most widely known, but that does not minimize the seriousness of the others. Each, in its own way, can be extremely debilitating, sometimes even life-threatening, to the individual who suffers from it. Whatever type of condition is producing the sleep disorder, it should be realized that such situations are not to be taken lightly or dismissed without proper medical consultation.

Sleep is essential to our well-being, and conditions that inhibit sound, restful sleep can produce far-ranging side effects.

Periodic Limb Movement Disorder

Just before falling asleep, many people feel an uncomfortable, not always painful, sensation deep in their thighs, calves and/or feet. Vigorous movement usually eases it enough for the sufferers to get to sleep, but the next day they may feel sleepy and fatigued. Sometimes, they may complain of an "itching, crawling sensation in their legs, as if a current were running through them."

People suffering from periodic limb movement disorder, also known as restless leg syndrome, experience irritability, a lack of motivation, poor job performance, and difficulty maintaining appropriate relationships within the family or society as a whole.

What happens is that these people have experienced repetitive jerks and twitches of the leg muscles, followed by literally hundreds of related awakenings throughout the night. Their restorative sleep, the slow-wave and REM portions of their sleep cycle, has been disturbed. The same symptoms can be experienced during the day, particularly when the sufferer is attempting to relax.

The condition is most common among those who are middle-aged and older. It is rare among children. It may be hereditary, or it might result from a variety of medical problems, such as kidney disease, withdrawal from certain medications, some metabolic disorders, diabetes, anemia, or disorders of the spinal or peripheral nerves. Pregnant women frequently develop it, but the symptoms usually disappear after delivery. Families may have a predisposition to suffer from the ailment. Studies also have shown that the condition may result from a shortage of Vitamin E, iron or calcium; and vitamin and mineral supplements are often prescribed. Sometimes leg exercises will produce a satisfactory cure; on other occasions, drugs may be required.

The ailment seems to affect men and women equally, and an attack can occur whenever the individual sits or lies down, although it is more frequent — and severe — at night.

Advanced Sleep Phase Syndrome

Those who suffer from ASPS have trouble staying awake in the evening, but awaken before the sun comes up. Friends may claim that "they have their days and nights mixed up," and indeed that is a fairly good description of their ailment.

Man lives on a planet where the day/night cycle lasts 24 hours. Nature has adapted him to that kind of cycle, and we talk about his circadian rhythms (the word *circadian* is from Latin and means "about a day"). People who suffer from ASPS have somehow gotten their circadian rhythms out of synchronization with their own wishes or with the cyclic standards of those around them.

ASPS is often found among those who spend a great deal of time indoors and those who live isolated lives. It affects up to one-third of our population and is common among the elderly.

People with ASPS often complain of digestive problems such as diarrhea, constipation, or ulcers; sensitivity to cold; muscle cramps, aches, and pains; and menstrual cycle disorders. They may experience decreased daytime alertness. Emotional problems and marital difficulties may arise. Many tend to over-use or abuse sleeping medications or alcohol.

One method of treatment, chronotherapy — time therapy — involves moving the patient's bedtime backwards around the clock in three-hour jumps every two days (for example) until the patient is readjusted to a more desirable bedtime.

A newer treatment, still under investigation, involves exposure in the evening to artificial lights several times brighter than ordinary room lights in order to help the body "reset" its circadian rhythms.

Bedwetting

Bedwetting (enuresis) is a common sleep disorder found in children. Between five and 17 percent of the children between three and five years of age wet their beds.

Although the condition usually ends by the time a child has reached the age of four or five, one out of three four-year-olds, one in ten six-year-olds, and one in twenty ten-year-olds continues to wet the bed. Bedwetting that continues into adolescence or adulthood may be attributed to emotional problems, but neurological disease or diabetes also can be the cause.

Very few cases (fewer than one percent) are emotionally or psychologically caused. Sometimes the culprit is a congenitally small bladder, a bladder infection, or some other physical problem.

Worry or embarrassment may keep a child from spending the night with a friend or from going away to camp, and may lower the child's self-esteem. For some children, the physician may recommend drugs or a short period of time away from home as a means of treatment.

Nightmares

Nightmares occur in all age groups, but are most common in children between the ages of three and six. They generally occur late in one's sleep, and they rarely prompt talking, screaming, striking out, or sleepwalking. Unlike sleep terrors, they generally can be recalled afterward and are accompanied by much less anxiety and movement. Nightmares tend to occur at times of insecurity, emotional turmoil, depression, or guilt.

REM Sleep Behavior Disorder

Ordinarily, the body lies virtually paralyzed during REM (rapid eye movement) sleep, which is the phase of sleep in which we tend to dream, but in people with this condition the normal paralysis of REM sleep fails and patients act out their dreams, frequently injuring themselves or their bed partners.

One man dreamed that his wife was a wild animal and tried to choke her. Another walked through a plate glass door, severing an artery.

Drs. Mark Mahowald and Carlos Schenck of the Minnesota Regional Sleep Disorders Center at Hennepin County Medical Center in Minneapolis identified this condition in 1986. Most of those who suffer from this ailment are men over fifty years of age.

The drug Clonazepam® improves the sleep of those who experience this condition and seems to eliminate the dream disturbances.

Sleep Terrors

Most common among children between the ages of four and twelve (where it is known as *Pavor nocturnus*), attacks of this sleeping disorder usually occur during the first third of the night.

Typically, the child will scream and sit upright in bed, flushed and sweating, but not awake. The child will look frightened and will breathe heavily. Attempts to comfort the child will go unnoticed, and if awakened, the child may appear confused, disoriented, and unable to recount the "bad dream." Usually, the child will have no recollection of the episode in the morning.

The ailment seems to be more common in boys than in girls, and usually disappears as the child grows older. It does not indicate a personality disorder, but it may progress into sleepwalking over a period of time.

Sleepwalking

A person who suffers attacks of sleepwalking (somnambulism) typically sits up, gets out of bed, and moves about in an uncoordinated manner. Less often, he may dress, open doors, eat, or go to the bathroom without incident. Sometimes, however, a sleepwalker may injure himself by stumbling against furniture, falling through a window, or tumbling downstairs.

The dangers of sleepwalking are related to lack of waking judgment. One woman made her way to the kitchen, opened the refrigerator, and then prepared and ate a "snack" of buttered cigarettes and cat food sandwiches. Another woman awoke while struggling to open a bottle of ammonia cleaning fluid, which she had planned to drink. A fourteen-year-old boy got up, walked to the refrigerator, and then stepped out the door — of the family camper, which was going fifty miles per hour on the San Diego Freeway. The sleepwalker is notoriously hard to arouse. One patient went so far as to tie one end of a rope around his waist and the other end to his bed, hoping that the weight of the bed would tug him awake if he began to wander. Instead, he sleepwalked anyway, laboriously towing the bed behind him. (In the Parks-Woods murder case, described in Chapter 1, even deep knife wounds did not awaken the sleepwalker.)

Sleepwalkers may rearrange the furniture, press against a wall as if to hold it up, or gather dirty clothes — which they carefully place in the oven. They also may engage in totally inappropriate behavior, such as urinating in a closet. Many have driven themselves around the neighborhood while asleep.

Sleepwalkers are *not* acting out their dreams; sleepwalking is distinct from dreaming.

An adult sleepwalker often becomes extremely angry when frustrated, and directs his anger outward at the world, rather than inward at himself.

The typical sleepwalking episode begins about three hours after the individual has fallen asleep and lasts for five to fifteen minutes. The sleepwalker's eyes generally are held extremely wide open and staring, and the pupils are dilated.

Sleepwalking is most frequent in children between the ages of four and eight. Forty percent of the children sleepwalk at some time, but children generally outgrow the tendency by the time they reach adolescence.

Among adults, men and women are equally affected. The condition seems to afflict between one and two percent of our population.

In adults, sleepwalking may indicate a personality disturbance. The condition seems to be, at least in part, hereditary. Stress, getting too little sleep, or a fever may act to bring on an episode. Many sleepwalkers suffer from depression.

Some individuals engage in sleep "talking." Such communication is very simple and the words may be repeated again and again. Such talk often is incomprehensible and rarely of psychological significance.

Sudden Infant Death Syndrome (SIDS)

In the tragic and largely inexplicable sleep-related phenomenon known as crib death or sudden infant death syndrome, the victim dies unexpectedly and suddenly. Thorough postmortem investigations have failed to demonstrate an adequate cause for death in these cases, at least 80 percent of which occur at a time when the infant was assumed to be asleep. It has not been established whether the primary cause of death is cardiac or respiratory failure.

Generally, SIDS victims were believed healthy immediately prior to death. Temporary association with a mild upper respiratory infection has been observed in about 60 percent of SIDS cases, but this cannot explain the death. Usually, death is the first sign of any problem.

Although infants who die of SIDS appear healthy prior to death, there are some infants at increased risk. These include:

> **Preterm Births.** Infants whose birth weight is below three pounds have a SIDS occurrence rate of eleven deaths per 1,000 live births. The risk is enhanced in proportion to immaturity.

> **Twins and triplets.** After the death due to SIDS of one member, not necessarily the smallest, the surviving infant is at higher risk than a single birth.

> **Subsequent Siblings of SIDS Victims.** Recently, better controlled studies have placed the increased risk for siblings at not more than two to four times the rate of the general population (1 or 2 per 1,000 live births). Subsequent siblings of two or more SIDS victims have a substantially increased SIDS risk.

> **Infants born to substance-abusing mothers.** Infants born to such mothers — especially those using opiates and cocaine —

are at as much as ten times the risk of the general population.

Children of Some Minority Groups. The SIDS rate is elevated in lower socioeconomic groups. Black and Eskimo babies are at four to six times increased risk for SIDS; the rate is lower when a correction is made for socioeconomic status.

The following factors also contribute to increased risk: teenage pregnancy, especially if coupled with several previous births; short interpregnancy interval; winter, spring, and fall births; and smoking during pregnancy. None of the described factors either singly or in combination permits accurate prediction of which infant will die of SIDS.

SIDS is rarely seen during the first week of life; the rate increases sharply after that time and reaches a peak between ten and twelve weeks of age. Ninety percent of SIDS deaths occur before six months of age. Fewer than one percent of SIDS deaths occur past the first birthday. Preterm infants die from SIDS later after birth than their full-term counterparts.

CHAPTER SIX

Insomnia Is Not a Disease!

The vast majority of us take sleep for granted. It is just something that we do, like eating or taking a shower. But — as we have learned — getting a good night's sleep is a problem of major proportions for a substantial part of our population.

Insomnia

The form that sleep problems take for the great majority of sleep sufferers is called *insomnia* — the inability to fall asleep, stay asleep, or to sleep well. It is safe to say that almost all of us suffer from it in one form or another at some time in our lives.

Some people are inclined to suffer insomnia during times of stress, much as other people might suffer headaches or indigestion. A troubled marriage, a sick child, or an unrewarding job can often disrupt people's sleep. However, we tend to be troubled by the unusual, the uncommon, the unfamiliar things that occur in our lives — and so, passing changes in our sleep patterns may alarm us.

Remember when you were a child and Christmas, a birthday or some other special event was approaching? Did you have trouble getting to sleep the night before? Most people have had that experience. In fact, it is the principle theme of Clement C. Moore's delightful ballad "A Visit From St. Nicholas," which begins: "'Twas the night before Christmas/ and all through the house/ not a creature was stirring,/ not even a mouse." The eve of a major examination in class, one's first school prom, high school or college graduation, marriage, the birth of a child — all of these and many other special events are frequently the occasions for attacks of insomnia.

The effects of insomnia are predictable. If sleep is reduced to five hours per night, even if only for a span of two nights, alertness, vigilance, and creativity all suffer. Sleepy people are less ambitious and less productive. Their performance on cognitive tasks involving memory, learning, logical reasoning, arithmetic calculations, pattern recognition, complex verbal processing, and decision-making has been shown to be impaired by sleep loss.

Still, most of us will find that with the passing of the external event that has caused the insomnia, or with some simple changes in habit, regular sleep returns. However, for some, the solution is less simple.

Insomnia, then, is a *symptom,* not an illness. It is a condition in which people frequently are unable to get to sleep for as much as an hour after they turn in, awaken frequently during the night, or awaken early and are unable to go back to sleep.

Insomnia can be short-term, lasting no more than a few days (*transient* insomnia), or long-term, lasting indefinitely. Obviously, the form that we experience as children waiting anxiously for tomorrow to arrive is transient or short-term insomnia.

Common causes of transient insomnia are such things as a cold, a headache, a toothache, bruised muscles, or indigestion. Most people do not sleep as well for the first night or two away from home. Too vigorous an athletic workout also can temporarily disrupt one's sleep.

Long-term insomnia, however, can be serious enough to radically degrade the quality of the sufferer's life. This is how one woman suffering from insomnia described its effects:

I had a major breakdown due to insomnia, work overload and other emotional problems. I had to take time off my job to try to recover, but recovery eluded me, and the job I loved drifted daily ever further out of reach. With the loss of the job came fears of financial difficulties. Being helpless to reverse the trend, I became despondent. Being alive was impossible; life had become a living hell. The sleepless nights continued along with the horror-filled days, and the tensions in our home reached the place where my husband could no longer cope and he considered divorce. The insomnia had worn me down to the point where I couldn't take care of myself. . . . I was really scared that I'd never be able to pick up the pieces of my life, and would have to sit an emotional, sleepless cripple for the rest of my life.

What Causes Insomnia?

Researchers speculate that the body produces a sleep-inducing chemical, as yet unidentified, that accumulates while we are awake. As the chemical builds up over a period of time, we become sleepier and sleepier, and we eventually doze off.

Some of this activity within our bodies is governed by our "biological clocks," which are located in our brains. These "clocks" control the time at which we go to sleep and the time at which we awake. The major periods of sleepiness occur between 2:00 and 8:00 A.M. and again shortly after lunch. In some cultures, the latter period of drowsiness is often accommodated by a siesta; in our culture, people are more inclined to turn to coffee.

However, a number of conditions — both internal and external — can cause this process to go awry.

Sometimes, pregnancy brings on insomnia.

Women are more likely to suffer from insomnia than men by a ratio of 40 percent to 30 percent.

Appetite suppressants are well known for their tendency to suppress sleep as well.

Smokers take longer to fall asleep and sleep more lightly than those who do not smoke.

Shift workers have more trouble with insomnia than others. Between 40 percent and 80 percent of them say they have difficulty sleeping. Little wonder: the average shift worker sleeps between two and four hours less each night than the day worker.

The elderly are half again as likely to suffer from insomnia.

Beta-blockers (Atenolol®, Nadolol®, Propranolol® and others) often used in the treatment of hypertension can cause disturbing dreams and a subsequent wakefulness.

Anxiety, nervousness, and physical or mental tension also are common causes of transient, or passing, insomnia. Insomnia caused by anxiety may stem from the illness of a loved one, a pending divorce, uncertainty over approval of a home loan, or the loss of a job. Insomnia caused by nervousness can result from something as minor as wondering who will win the World Series, or going in for a job interview, or preparing to ask someone out on a first date.

Financial or marital problems are a common cause of transient insomnia. Excessive concern about your health, boredom, social isolation, and physical confinement also can bring on transient insomnia.

Insomnia is America's most common sleep complaint. It afflicts more than 60 million people — about one out of every three adults — and in about half of those individuals, the condition is severe. Most of the time, however, the distress is temporary, brought on by some sort of anxiety, such as a problem at work, a sudden family crisis, or a financial situation.

Delayed Sleep Phase Syndrome

One of the conditions commonly referred to as insomnia is one that the sleep researchers call delayed sleep phase syndrome. Those who experience it generally go to bed late, have difficulty falling asleep, and then sleep late in the morning.

Victims of this disorder normally are teenagers or young adults, particularly college students. Often, they suffer from fatigue throughout the day due to the loss of sleep that was suffered the night before.

Pain, fever, itching, and coughing often contribute to the disorder, but many of the drugs necessary to treat those problems also tend to disrupt one's sleep. Usually, those who are bothered by this condition will be able to get an adequate amount of sleep if they are allowed to retire later at night and rise later in the morning.

Learned Insomnia

As strange as it may seem, there is one form of insomnia that its sufferers "acquire," usually as the result of a traumatic event, such as the death of a loved one. Due to the emotional trauma they have experienced, these people have difficulty falling asleep. This is not an unusual occurrence throughout the population as a whole, under such circumstances. As a rule, one adjusts to the trauma and the ability to fall asleep at night usually returns.

Those who suffer from this disorder, however, focus intently upon their inability to fall asleep, rather than on the trauma that caused it. As worry about not falling asleep becomes a fixation with them, it actually becomes a self-fulfilling prophesy. They literally *convince* themselves that they cannot fall asleep and that belief eventually turns into a reality.

Jet Lag and Insomnia

The jet lag that many people experience after a rapid change in time zones is a form of transient insomnia. Crossing a number of time zones while on a trip imbalances our circadian rhythms. Our meals, our activities, and our sleep habits no longer coincide with our customary routine. Environmental cues, especially daylight, are no longer synchronized to our internally-generated rhythms, causing us to have trouble sleeping, experience sleepiness during the daytime, suffer gastrointestinal problems, and be troubled by a reduced attention span. It can impair both our physical and mental performance.

Even a one-hour time shift may require at least a day for complete readjustment.

The severity of the condition generally depends on how many time zones were crossed, whether the traveler was headed east or west, age, and various individual differences. To overcome the debilitating effects of jet lag, try these tips:

> Drink plenty of water, fruit juices or other non-carbonated beverages before and during the flight. Avoid alcohol, caffeine and smoking.

> Take off your shoes as soon as the plane is airborne.

> Stretch and move about the plane periodically.

> Assume the activity schedule of the people at your destination as soon as you arrive.

Using a mild sleeping medication for a day or two may help some people.

Usually, it takes our bodies about a day to adjust to each time zone that we have passed through. Getting the entire system back into synchronization may take as many as twelve days after a nine-hour flight across several time zones.

Long-term Insomnia Is More Complex

The causes of long-term insomnia usually are more complex and often more difficult to determine. For example, long-term insomnia may be caused by something as mundane as the environment.

More than 35 million Americans suffer from chronic insomnia and experience poor sleep every night, on most nights, or at least on several nights of the month. Their insomnia can last for months — or years. It may be the result of an organic illness or the symptom of an underlying psychiatric problem.

Ten to 15 percent of the patients who have chronic insomnia suffer from underlying substance abuse. Some 18 million people over the age of 18 in America are alcoholics or problem drinkers.

Those who live on a busy street, by a school or near an airport may have trouble sleeping and never realize what is causing their problem. Once they discover the cause, they can easily cure their insomnia by simply moving to a quieter neighborhood.

Insomniacs often attempt to medicate themselves through the use of drugs or alcohol. Chronic alcohol or drug abuse actually can bring about long-term insomnia, as can the excessive use of caffeine or the abuse of sleeping pills. Curtailing the use of these drugs generally will cure the insomnia.

Pills: A "Catch 22"

The use of sleep-inducing drugs can become a double-edged sword. Individuals who develop some sort of sleeping problem will often respond by taking a sleeping tablet. In short order, the drug may be causing more problems than it was intended to cure.

Needless to say, one should *always* consult a physician before taking a sleeping pill of any sort. Such pills should never be taken for longer than two or three weeks and can lose their effectiveness with time. There often is a tendency to take higher and higher doses of the drug as its effectiveness diminishes, and this has frequently brought about a drug dependency.

All sleeping pills depress the nervous system in order to put the user to sleep. Not all sleeping pills are alike, however. Most of them fall into the categories of hypnotics, barbiturates or benzodiazepines, plus a variety of prescription and over-the-counter medicatons.

Barbiturates. Barbiturates such as phenobarbital and pentobarbital usually lose their effectiveness after two or three weeks of continuous use, and doctors today tend not to recommend them.

Benzodiazepines. Hypnotics such as Valium®, Dalmane®, Halcion® and Prozac® can be dangerous, particularly if taken in combination with alcohol or if taken in excess by someone with a respiratory disorder. Some forms of the drug can aid in inducing sleep for up to thirty days — but not all of them work alike. Some work faster than others, some produce longer-lasting effects, and some are eliminated from the body more rapidly than others. If you are taking one of these drugs, follow your physician's advice carefully.

Over-the-Counter Medications. Over the past ten years, the number of drug store prescriptions for sleeping pills has been cut in half. Doctors today tend to prescribe pills for only 10 percent of their patients suffering from insomnia. However, another 5 percent of those patients buy non-prescription, over-the-counter drugs, and still others unwisely use drugs that are intended for some other purpose, such as an antihistamine, an anticholinergic drug or a tranquilizer. Only a physician can tell you what drug is best suited for your particular form of insomnia. One might be best for helping you to fall asleep; another, for stemming anxiety, if that is what is causing your insomnia; and another, for helping you to maintain a sound sleep throughout the night. Some conditions simply cannot be treated with drugs.

Using drugs to help solve a sleeping problem can lead to other difficulties, such as inducing a disturbed sleep, creating uncomfortable side effects, causing a sleep "hangover" during the day, and even drug dependence. Drugs can be fatal when taken with alcohol or other drugs; and they should never be taken by those who intend to drive an automobile or operate any other type of machinery.

Under the most severe circumstances, sleeping medications should be used *sparingly,* for the *shortest possible* period of time, and in the *smallest dosage* that proves effective.

It bears repeating that sleeping potions offer only limited usefulness and should be taken only when one's health, safety or well-being are at risk. They should never be taken without consulting a physician.

After the use of drugs has been discontinued, a sleeping disorder often tends to return, sometimes even worse than before.

The solution to a sleeping problem is *to locate the cause of the problem and to cure it,* not to frustrate yourself with an often futile attempt to cure the symptoms.

Medical Problems and Long-term Insomnia

Generally, long-term insomnia stems from some medical problem. Heart disease, arthritis, diabetes, asthma, chronic sinusitis, epilepsy and ulcers can often lead to insomnia. Stroke, dementia, chronic pain, Parkinson's disease, Alzheimer's disease, and other disorders of the central nervous system can affect — and be affected by — sleep.

Asthma is a common respiratory condition that is often associated with nocturnal symptoms. Asthma attacks worsen during sleep in many cases. A recent study shows that 39 percent of the patients under examination reported respiratory symptoms every night and 64 percent reported such symptoms at least three times a week. The number of deaths due to asthma continues to climb — and 70 percent of those deaths occur during normal sleeping hours.

About 60 to 90 percent of the patients seeking medical treatment for Parkinson's disease complain of poor sleep, yet sleep disturbances and subsequent daytime dysfunction are not even mentioned in neurology textbooks as a symptom of the disease.

Thrombotic disease, clotting in the blood vessels, is more likely to occur during sleep or upon awakening. It has been indicated as a major cause of strokes, which occur most frequently at those times, and heart attacks, which seem to occur most often around 9:00 A.M.

There is a definite interaction between sleep and epileptic seizures. Seizures may lead to chronic sleep deprivation, and that in turn may make the seizures even worse.

Physical problems, particularly painful ones like arthritis, angina, ulcers, or migraine headaches, often interfere with sleep. Chronic lung, kidney or thyroid disorders also often result in interrupted sleep.

It is speculated that sleep may even affect the body's immune system.

Psychiatric Conditions and Insomnia

Psychiatric conditions ranging from simple depression to schizophrenia also can bring on insomnia. Forty-seven percent of those who suffer from severe insomnia also report a high level of emotional stress. The relationship between the two is easy to understand.

Some 16 million Americans suffer from anxiety disorders, the most prevalent mental health problem in the country. Depression and substance abuse often co-exist in these illnesses, and insomnia is a common complaint. About three percent of the population suffers from chronic low-grade depression called dysthymia, which is characterized by periods of too much sleep and, less commonly, too little sleep.

People troubled by anxiety, by a phobia of some sort, by an obsession, or by a compulsion may be awakened by nightmares and feelings of sadness, conflict or guilt. Concerns regarding these things can so dominate their minds that their sleep can be delayed, disturbed or shortened as a result.

Waking earlier than desired in the morning is one of the most common symptoms of depression, and disturbed sleep is a prominent feature of the manic-depressive, of which there are approximately one million in the United States.

Sleep disturbances may be a hallmark of post-traumatic stress disorder, a form of anxiety that affects as many as 20 percent of our wounded Vietnam veterans as well as those who suffer from some other type of traumatic experience, such as sexual abuse or being involved in some natural disaster.

Panic disorder, which is characterized by periods of intense fear of the discomfort associated with chest pain, rapid and pounding heartbeats, and sweating that unexpectedly occur, afflicts two percent of all Americans. There is no known medical cause.

According to a study conducted by the National Institute of Mental Health, 40 percent of those who have insomnia (too little sleep) and 47 percent of those who have hypersomnia (too much sleep) suffer from a mental disorder. Among those who have no sleep disorder, the figure is about16 percent.

Some people are *chronically tense,* and are so restless, so hyperactive or so apprehensive that they actually *expect* not to sleep when they go to bed.

Those who are depressed can experience overwhelming feelings of sadness, hopelessness, worthlessness or guilt, and these can effect their ability to sleep. Such people often wake up early and cannot go back to sleep. On the other hand, some of those who suffer from this kind of depression tend to react in the opposite manner, using sleep as a refuge from their problems and therefore sleeping excessively.

Other people, such as those who seem to have lost their sense of purpose in life, will frequently report an overwhelming urge to sleep, a constant feeling of being tired, and sleep that is marked by an irregular sleep/wake pattern.

Eighty percent of the homeless questioned during a recent study complained that they experience severe sleep disturbances and daytime sleepiness.

Those who find that they have lost interest in activities that they once enjoyed, who experience feelings of hopelessness, or who have suicidal thoughts also tend to become victims of insomnia — and should consult a physician, who may recommend psychiatric consultation. It is the depression that underlies such feelings that needs treatment, not the insomnia. On occasion, anti-depressant drugs or psychotherapy may be required to help the patient through an episode of serious depression.

CHAPTER SEVEN

What Would You Do For a Good Night's Sleep?

I t is unfortunate, but important facts about sleep are not taught in public or private schools, medical schools, residencies, nursing schools, or even continuing medical education programs. They are not widely disseminated in books or magazine articles. Most general practitioners are not familiar with them.

The only recourse most individuals have is to do some research on their own — and that is the primary purpose of this book.

At the very least when you are well rested, you should be alert enough to read a daily newspaper or watch a television program without dozing off. You should be able to stay awake in school or on the job without difficulty or risk of injury. You should also be able to drive a car without danger to yourself or others. If you can't do these basic tasks, then you may have a real medical problem and need to see a doctor or sleep specialist.

Through the previous chapters, we have tried to suggest certain warning signals that should prompt you to seek competent medical counsel. The most common one, of course, is a persistent daytime drowsiness that prevents you from living life as you would like to live it. Obviously, there are a lot of other indicators, some equally obvious and some much more subtle. When in doubt, consult your physician.

Real breakthroughs will come only through competent biomedical research, however. Powerful new techniques such as brain imaging, molecular biological tools, and neurochemical analysis should be used in human studies and animal models to explore the basic mechanisms of sleep and sleep disorders.

Diet and Sleep

Can Mashed Potates Make You Sleepy?

For years, studies have suggested that tryptophan, an amino acid that occurs naturally in food, may help to promote sleep. Foods that are high in carbohydrates increase the level of tryptophan in the blood. Protein-rich foods tend to decrease it.

This is because protein is rich in many amino acids, among them tryptophan, and the presence of the other amino acids may interefere with the ability of tryptophan to cross the "blood-brain barrier" and enter the brain. On the other hand, when you eat foods rich in carbohydrates, the body produces a wealth of insulin, which is needed to digest carbohydrates. This insulin also transports most amino acids — except tryptophan — to the skeletal muscles. When insulin is busy performing this task, tryptophan has little competition and can easily enter the brain, where it joins with serotonin to regulate sleep patterns.

Tryptophan is marketed in pill form in some health food stores. In large doses, it tends to cause nausea; in doses low enough to be tolerated, it seems to work best in people with only mild cases of insomnia. Few researchers, however, believe that the substance will ever play more than an ancillary role in relieving insomnia.

Still, some sufferers of insomnia have reported that they sleep better after drinking that classic remedy, a glass of milk (which contains trytophan) — and some researchers have substantiated this. Whether the milk is hot or not depends on your taste. Some people enjoy a bedtime mug of hot milk stirred with a tablespoonful of honey and topped with a sprinkling of grated nutmeg.

The sum of these findings suggests that you may find it sleep-inducive to include foods high in complex carbohydrates such as potatoes, pasta, corn, and bread in your evening meal.

During the day, eat high-protein foods (fish, lean meat, nuts, legumes) to keep you alert, and avoid high-carbohydrate meals that can induce drowsiness. In one study, subjects given a high-carbohydrate meal performed less efficiently at a task requiring sustained attention than those given a high-protein meal. A related study found that children who missed breakfast showed decreased cognitive performance. This suggests that regular meals containing some protein may assist with learning and thinking, and that less protein and more carbohydrate is the best balance for meals taken before sleep.

Another Hot Cup of Coffee

The caffeine consumed daily by Americans in 1979 equalled approximately the amount found in a cup and a half of coffee. Some came from coffee and some from soft drinks. A soft drink contains about the same amount of caffeine as a half cup of coffee. It is well known that caffeine interferes with sleep for most people. It should also be noted that caffeine taken by a nursing mother in any form — coffee, chocolate, soft drinks, or tea — is secreted in breast milk. Infants eliminate caffeine poorly. Therefore significant amounts of caffeine can accumulate in the infants of nursing mothers who take caffeine — perhaps resulting in sleep problems.

In general, do not drink coffee, tea, or cola after dinner — or for some sensitive persons, after lunch. It takes three hours for one cup of coffee to leave your system.

Sugar and Sleep

If you wish to eat sweets, do so at the end of the work shift and not just before bedtime. An influx of simple carbohydrates — from sugar —

into the bloodstream has a complicated effect on the body, especially in women. In many it can cause an immediate "sugar high" as insulin pours into the system, resulting in a later "sugar dip" as the body experiences a rebound effect. Both aspects of the sugar cycle can interfere with sleep.

Don't Smoke and Beware of Alcohol Consumption

Nicotine is even worse than caffeine for preventing the onset of sleep, and consumption of substantial amounts of alcohol can seriously disrupt the normal sleep cycle.

Time Your Feasting Appropriately

Both going to bed hungry and consuming a large meal just before bedtime can inhibit sleep. If you feel hungry at bedtime, eat a light snack or drink a glass of warm milk.

Medication

Before taking any medication, have a doctor look at your medical history and give you a complete physical examination. Self-medicating a sleeping problem with alcohol or an over-the-counter sleep preparation should be avoided as they can often produce unpleasant, even harmful, side effects.

The active ingredients in over-the-counter sleep aids are antihistamines, for example. Antihistamines were developed to treat allergies and they only produce drowsiness as a side effect. Those with the greatest sedative effect are Nytol®, Sleep-Eze 3®, Sominex® and others containing diphenhydramine, which also is an effective cough suppressant; and Unisom®, which contains doxylamine. Quiet World® and other drugs containing pyrilamine generally produce less drowsiness, but create more stomach upset.

Individual response to these over-the-counter drugs varies widely. Some people — usually children, but some older people as well — become aroused, rather than sleepy.

Sudafed® (pseudoephedrine) has a stimulating effect. Dristan® (an antihistamine) causes drowsiness.

If you take any of these medications, read the directions on the package carefully. Most, if not all of them, will warn you against driving when you are taking the medication; heed that warning religiously.

Prescription sleeping drugs include barbiturates such as phenobarbital and products like Seconal®, which contains secobarbital.

Today, however, the drugs of choice seem to be the benzodiazepines, which are safer and more effective. This actually is a family of drugs, rather than a single drug. It includes Librium®, which contains chlordiazepoxide; Valium®, which contains diazepam; Dalmane®, which contains flurazepam; Restoril®, which contains temazepam; and Halcion®, which contains triazolam. All but Halcion are available generically.

Halcion, it should be noted, is a highly controversial drug. It has been banned in Great Britain, and has been cited by one woman as the drug that caused the death of her son. It was used with bad side effects by actor Burt Reynolds and is blamed for the collapse of President George Bush during his visit to Japan.

Like alcohol, sleeping pills interfere with normal sleep patterns by suppressing the dreaming stage of sleep. Do NOT take sleeping pills after drinking alcohol.

Current recommendations call for taking a sleeping pill for a night or two, then skipping a night or two. One should not take them every night. Sleeping pills usually are not prescribed for more than three weeks' time.

Some prescription medicines, including several that control high blood pressure, can block sleep.

Hypnotic medications should not be the mainstay in a course of treatment for insomnia. They are overused and have the potential to become habit-forming.

About 4.3 percent of our population is given prescription medication for some sleep disorder each year. That's 24 million prescriptions per year! Millions more take over-the-counter sleep medication, although fortunately about three-fourths of them take it for less than two weeks.

If you are having trouble sleeping, avoid diet pills and any over-the-counter pain, cold or allergy medicines that contain stimulants.

Nighttime Tips

Most people find that following these tips results in better, more regular sleep.

Develop a variety of interests.

Don't nap during the day. Try going shopping instead.

Relax before bedtime, perhaps by reading or with a little music.

Don't spend too much time in bed chasing sleep.

Keep regular bedtime and rising hours.

Eat meals at the same time each day, every day. It helps to regulate the body's internal clock.

Take an hour or so to relax after work. Relaxing music or a warm bath may help.

Set aside some specific "worry time," but not too close to bedtime. Get the day's problems out of the way *before* you turn in.

Plan evening activities that are conducive to relaxation.

Develop a sleep ritual. Do the same things each evening before turning in to give your body cues that it is time to settle down.

Lie down intending to sleep only when you are sleepy.

Take several deep breaths while lying in bed and progressively relax tense muscles, starting with your toes and working up to your head.

If you can't fall asleep, get up and go to another room. When you are sleepy, return to your bed. If you still can't fall sleep, get up again.

Set your alarm and get up at the same time each morning, regardless of how much sleep you got during the night.

Don't try to make up for lost sleep on weekends or holidays.

Changes in your daily pattern of living will affect your family, too. Include your family in your planning.

Keep Your Body in Action for Health, for Sleep

Exercise. Take a long walk after dinner. Late afternoon and early evening are the best times for taking a walk. If it's raining, some light stretching may be sufficient. Do not exercise too strenuously, however, as too much activity shortly before bedtime can be too stimulating.

On coffee breaks at work, walk around. Physical activity promotes wakefulness.

If persistent yawning occurs, straighten your posture, take a few deep breaths, and walk around. Physical activity promotes air intake and benefits mental alertness.

Breathe deeply to induce drowsiness. Taking a series of three very slow, deep breaths, exhaling fully each time, helps to break tension.

More Dos and Don'ts

Sleep in a good bed — a comfortable bed— and use it only for sleep and sex.

Don't use your bed as a place to read, watch TV, eat, argue, or catch up on your office work.

Keep the bedroom dark and cool (64 to 66 degrees).

Block out noises that can disturb your sleep. If necessary, block out disturbing sounds with the use of sponge earplugs or "white noise" (made by fans, air conditioners, and the like).

Before You Turn Out the Lights. . .

We wish you good night, sweet dreams, and restful slumber. May peace, like sleep, "that knits up the ravel'd sleave of care," be upon you. And if you cannot find the rest you need, may you find the strength and clarity to seek it through counsel with a good physician or other specialist who can help you break the sleep deprivation that undermines your safety, happiness, and productivity and that of those near you.

Appendices

Appendix I:

A Recommendation from the National Commission on Sleep Disorders

We do not know enough about normal sleep. Our understanding of the causes of and solutions to sleep disorders is fragile. Research is severely limited, both by the absolute number of sleep researchers in the field and by an inadequate, decentralized funding system. A very small amount of money is being spent on sleep research. In Fiscal Year 1990, the monetary commitment of the federal government to research directed at certain ailments shows sleep lagging way behind:

For AIDS, the research funds set aside in 1990 amounted to $1,695 million; for cancer $1,580 million; for heart disease $704 million; for Alzheimer's Disease $153 million. But for sleep disorders, just $44 million was set aside for research.

Just as research into Alzheimer's disease has doubled over the past few years along with the federal government's commitment to scientific investigation of the disorder, so could a research program directed toward sleep disorders flourish — if the government would make a similar commitment to it.

Only one grant for insomnia research was funded by the National Institutes of Health in 1990. Pharmaceutical companies provide the only other significant source of funding for research related to insomnia. The National Institutes of Health do not fund a single investigator to work on fundamental mechanisms of sleep equilibrium in animals. Only two laboratories have grants to study sleepiness in humans. There is no basic research on genetics and sleep, only one $35,000 award on the phylogeny of sleep, no research on sleep and exercise, and no research on the epidemiology of sleep disorders.

Basic research on motor control during sleep, while receiving modest funding, mainly involves REM sleep, whereas the majority of the movement disorders involve non-REM sleep.

There is only one training program dedicated specifically to basic sleep research: the Multisite Basic Sleep Research Training Program based at UCLA and funded by the National Institute of Mental Health. The program supports the training of 10 predoctoral students and six postdoctoral students. The doctoral degree is granted in Neuroscience. There are fewer than 20 tenured scientists in the country pursuing basic sleep research.

Further complicating the issue is the lack of a well-defined career path in sleep research. Young people get no exposure whatever to sleep medicine and sleep research while they are making their career decisions.

Dr. William C. Dement, Chairman of the National Commission on Sleep Disorders Research and Director of the Stanford Sleep Disorders Clinic and Research Center, says that extremely important research is not getting done because of a lack of focus. There is simply a lack of a clear, designated responsibility and accountability for sleep disorders research, claims Dement.

Federal Action Plan Needed to Wake Up America

The National Commission on Sleep Disorders Research has submitted a long-term plan and recommendations to Congress. Things that need to be done immediately include:

1. Congress should authorize the establishment of a national center for research and education on sleep and sleep disorders, to be housed within an existing Institute within the National Institutes of Health. The center's activities should complement the research related to sleep and sleep disorders currently undertaken by the various NIH and ADAMHA Institutes and, through its own award authority, should encourage and support gap-filling and cross-cutting research, while developing new research programs and educational/training initiatives in the field.

2. Specifically identified offices on sleep and sleep disorders should

be established within all federal departments and agencies whose programs affect or are affected by issues of sleep and sleep disorders. The Office of Science Technology Policy should undertake a feasibility study for the establishment of a special body to ensure coordination and cooperation among the separate agency-based sleep/sleep disorder offices.

3. Federal support for basic, clinical, epidemiological, and health services research on sleep and sleep disorders should be expanded. Existing research commitments by the National Institute of Health and the Alcohol, Drug Abuse and Mental Health Association, as well as the Veterans Administration, the Department of Defense, and other federal agencies currently engaged in sleep and sleep disorders research should be strengthened.

4. Substantially increased levels of federal support should be directed to the NIH and ADAMHA Institutes as well as to the VA and DOD specifically for sleep and sleep disorder research training and career development opportunities.

5. Congress should encourage and support broader awareness of and training in sleep and sleep disorders spanning the full range of healthcare professionals, particularly at the primary care level.

6. A major public awareness education campaign about sleep and sleep disorders must be undertaken immediately by the federal government.

These initiatives will not necessarily lead to the total elimination of sleep disorders, but they will go a long way — particularly toward the all-important goal of increasing the general awareness of these issues by the public and by those who provide primary health care services.

However, nothing will happen if the congress does not take the action needed to enact the legislation and appropriate the funds necessary to implement the recommendations of the commission. There are many demands for federal funds; all compete against those needed for sleep disorders research programs. Every citizen must do his/her part to see that the National Commission on Sleep Disorders Research recommendations are adopted by congress.

Here's what you should do right now: Write a letter to each of your senators and congressional representatives urging them to support the implementation of the recommendations of the National Commission on Sleep Disorders Research. Send your letter to members of the Senate: The Honorable John Doe, The United States Senate, Washington, D.C. 20510. And to members of the House: The Honorable John Doe, U.S. House of Representatives, Washington, D.C. 20515.

By the time a sleep disorder affects you directly, it may be too late!

Appendix II

Glossary of Terms

Advanced sleep phase syndrome: A disorder in which falling asleep and waking occur earlier than usual; it is caused by an alteration in the individual circadian cycle and occurs most commonly among the elderly.

Altitude insomnia: Sleep problems experienced when rapidly relocating to a high altitude — for example, on a skiing or mountain climbing trip.

Apnea: A condition involving frequently interrupted breathing usually accompanied by heavy snoring and restless sleep.

Biological rhythm: Self-sustained, cyclic change in a physiological process or behavioral function of an organism that repeats at regular intervals. *See circadian rhythm, infradian rhythm, ultradian rhythm.*

Body clock: The internal mechanism of the body that controls biological rhythms.

Bright light: As it relates to circadian rhythms, light with an intensity of atleast 2.5000 lux, which is equivalent to outdoor light at dawn. Bright light has been shown to shift circadian rhythms and has been used to treat seasonal affective disorder, some sleep disorders, and jet lag.

Cataplexy: Sudden partial or complete loss of muscle tone concurrent with sudden emotional responses such as laughter, anger, surprise, or joy.

Circadian: About a day.

Circadian cycle: The 24-hour interval between recurrences of a defined phase of a circadian rhythm. *See circadian rhythm.*

Circadian rhythm: A self-sustained biological rhythm which in an organism's natural environment is normally synchronized to a 24-hour period. *See biological rhythm.*

Circadian rhythm disruption: Disorganization among an organism's internal cycles or desynchrony between self-generated rhythms and the 24-hour cycle in the environment.

Cortisol: A steroid hormone secreted by humans. Cortisol secretion exhibits a circadian rhythm and is used as a marker for the body's pacemaker.

Delayed sleep phase syndrome: Abnormal delay of the timing of sleep onset and waking, possibly caused by an abnormally long circadian cycle or a diminished responsiveness to environmental cues. Common among teenagers and young adults.

Dementia: A condition of deteriorated mentality.

Evening person: A general term used to describe an individual who has difficulty waking up, is able to sleep late in the morning, and finds it difficult to fall asleep at night. Also called an "owl." *Compare to morning person.*

Fatigue: Weariness caused by physical or mental exertion.

Fibrositis syndrome: Disorder characterized by chronic fatigue, muscle aches, and constant tiredness.

Hallucination: Perception of objects, scenes, or circumstances with no reality.

Idiopathic hypersomnia: Persistent daytime sleepiness.

Idiopathic insomnia: Sleepiness with unknown cause or causes.

Inadequate sleep hygiene: Lack of a regular schedule for sleeping and awakening or lack of an appropriate place for sleeping, such as a quiet dark room.

Infradian rhythm: A biological rhythm with a cycle of more than 24 hours; for example the human menstrual cycle. *See biological rhythm; compare ultradian rhythm.*

Insomnia: Inability to obtain adequate sleep.

Irregular sleep-wake pattern: Variation from a normal 24-hour sleep-wake rhythm, for example during jet lag.

Jet lag: The malaise associated with travel across time zones; it results from conflict between the traveler's internal clock and the external rhythms in the new time zone.

Microsleep: Brief episode of sleep experienced by a person who is so tired that he or she cannot resist sleep.

Morning person: A general term used to describe an individual who wakes up easily, has difficulty sleeping late, and falls asleep quickly at night. Also called a "lark." *Compare evening person.*

Narcolepsy: A neurological disorder which results in bouts of extreme daytime sleepiness.

Night tremors: Severe nocturnal arousal usually occurring in the first three hours of sleep with episodes of intense anxiety, tachycardia, increased blood pressure, dilated pupils and sweating. Usually lasts about six minutes.

Nightmares: Disturbing dreams usually occurring late in the nightly sleep cycle and more frequent in children three to six and in adults experiencing unusual daytime stress.

Nocturnal: Being active at night.

Non-REM sleep: The four stages of sleep during which the sleeper does not experience rapid eye movement (REM) sleep. *See slow wave sleep, rapid eye movement (REM) sleep.*

Panic attacks: Episodes of shortness of breath, sweating, tachycardia, and extreme fear. Differs from night terrors because the patient is fully alert, aware of his or her surroundings, and will have a clear recall the next morning.

Periodic limb movement disorder: A disorder that causes repetitive jerks and twitches of the leg muscles during periods of attempted sleep or relaxation. Technically known as *nocturnal myoclonus.*

Pregnancy-associated sleep disorder: Excessive tiredness or sleepiness in pregnant women.

Psychophysiological insomnia: Insomnia related to mental illness such as simple depression or schizophrenia.

Rapid eye movement (REM) sleep: Stage of sleep during which the eyes move rapidly, though the eyelids are closed, and brain activity resembles that observed during wakefulness. Heart rate and respiration increase and become erratic and vivid dreams are frequent. REM sleep alternates with non-REM sleep in cycles lasting 90 to 100 minutes. *Compare slow wave sleep.*

Recurrent hypersomnia: Repeated and excessive daytime sleepiness. The two leading causes are sleep apnea and narcolepsy.

REM sleep behavior disorder: Failure of the natural paralysis that usually occurs during REM (rapid eye movement) sleep, resulting in the potential for persons to physically act out their dreams.

Seasonal affective disorder (SAD): Recurring autumn or winter depression that may be helped by treatment with bright light. Although SAD has not been proved to be a circadian rhythm disorder, it has been hypothesized that changes in circadian rhythms cause the disorder.

Shift work sleep disorder: Insomnia or other sleep disorders related to change from one circadian rhythm to another due to change in work hours.

Shift worker: A person who works a nonstandard schedule, that is, at variance with the usual eight o'clock or nine o'clock to five o'clock daytime work schedule and whose work hours may rotate or change periodically.

Sleep apnea syndrome: A condition in which a neuromuscular irregularity results in the partial closing of the nasal pharynx while one sleeps, usually resulting in heavy snoring.

Sleep debt: The state of chronic fatigue and sleepiness that results from the lack of sufficient sleep or disrupted sleep, particularly over a period of several days or weeks. *See fatigue, sleep deprivation.*

Sleep enuresis: Also called bedwetting. Incontinence during sleep.

Sleep deprivation: Extended periods of insufficient sleep usually related to occupational, educational, social, or family demands.

Sleep disorders centers: Places where sleep problems are diagnosed and treated. For information about the sleep disorders center nearest you, contact your personal physician or write or call the American Sleep Disorders Association, 604 Second Street Southwest, Rochester, Minnesota 55902. Telephone (507) 287-6006.

Sleep terrors: Episodes of fear and disorientation usually occuring in the first third of the night and most common among children aged four to twelve.

Sleepwalking: Ambulation during sleep.

Slow wave sleep: The stages of sleep during which the eyes do not move, heart rate and respiration are slow and steady, muscles show little movment, and dreams are infrequent. *Compare rapid eye movement (REM) sleep.*

Snoring: Sound made by air pouring through irregular and narrow opening in the throat and windpipe.

Stressor: A source of stress, such as disruption of circadian rhythms, fatigue and disruption of sleep, and social and domestic disturbances caused by shift work.

Sudden infant death syndrome (SIDS): Unexplained sudden death among infants; 80 percent of SIDS or "crib deaths" occur at a time when the infant was assumed to be asleep.

Tachycardia: Relatively rapid heart action or accelerated heart beats.

Time zone change (jet lag) syndrome: Insomnia related to change in time zones due to travel from one location to another.

Transient insomnia: Short-term trouble in sleeping (lasting three weeks or less) such as may be experienced during periods of stress or excitement.

Ultradian rhythm: A biological rhythm with a cycle of less than 24 hours; human sleep cycles and the release of some hormones are examples. *See biological rhythm; compare infradian rhythm.*

Appendix III

Resources for Additional Information on Sleep Disorders

For additional information about sleep and sleep disorders, contact:
The American Narcolepsy Association, Inc.
P. O. Box 26230
San Francisco, CA 94126-6230
Members include patients with narcolepsy, their families, friends, physicians, health professionals and researchers. Provides information about narcolepsy, support groups, physician referrals, advocacy for narcolepsy issues. Accepts donations for directed narcolepsy research programs.

The American Sleep Apnea Association
P. O. Box 3803
Charlottesville, VA 22903
Members include patients with sleep apnea syndrome. Provides research, training, education, and advocacy for health professionals and patients with sleep apnea.

The American Sleep Disorders Association (ASDA)
1610 14th Street N.W., Suite 300
Rochester, MN 55901
(507) 287-6006
Members include health professionals, physicians and researchers who specialize in sleep disorders medicine and research, publishes standards for sleep-related disorders in clinical medicine; accreditation of sleep disorders centers, education and training programs for sleep professionals. Publishes *Sleep* Journal, information on sleep disorders for patients and their families.

Coalition to Wake Up America
711 Second Street N.E., Suite 200
Washington, D. C. 20002
(202) 544-7499
Advocacy organization of professionals and citizens who support the
implementation by Congress of the recommendations of the National
Commission on Sleep Disorders Research.

National Commission on Sleep Disorders Research
Dr. Wiliam C. Dement, Chairman
Stanford Sleep Disorders Center
701 Welch Road, Suite 2226
Palo Alto, CA 94304
(415) 725-6484
Reports to Congress on the needs and priorities in the national plan
for sleep disorders research.

National Organization for Rare Diseases (NORD)
P .O. Box 8923
New Fairfield, CT 06812
(203) 746-6518
Information, advocacy and networking for many little-known disor-
ders which affect less than 200,000 persons in the U. S.

National Sleep Foundation
122 South Robertson Blvd., Suite 201
Los Angeles, CA 90048
(213) 288-0466
Members are medical professionals and researchers in sleep disorders
medicine and research. Provides information to health care providers,
patients, the media and governmental agencies. Supports training and
research. Maintains referral lists of accredited sleep disorders centers .

National SIDS Resource Center
8201 Greenboro Drive, Suite 600
McLean, VA 22102
(703) 821-8955
Provides information about Sudden Infant Death Syndrome (SIDS).

Sudden Infant Death Syndrome Alliance
10500 Little Patuxent Pkwy., Suite 420
Columia, MD 21044
(800) 221-SIDS
Provides information about Sudden Infant Death Syndrome (SIDS).

University of Illinois at Chicago
College of Nursing (M/C 802)
Center for Narcolepsy Research
845 South Damen Avenue
Chicago, IL 60612
(312) 996-5176
Provides information, nursing education and conferences on narcolepsy; maintains support groups for narcolepsy patients and their families; quality of life surveys and research using state-of-the-art pupillometry equipment for measurement of sleepiness in adolescents. Accepts donations for narcolepsy research.

Appendix IV

Bibliography

Dement, William C., M.D. *The Sleepwatchers,* Stanford Alumni Association, Stanford, California, 1992.

Kutscher, Austin H. (editor). *Loss, Grief and Care,* The Haworth Press, Inc., Binghampton, New York, 1992.

Mitler, Elizabeth A. and Merrill M. *101 Questions About Sleep and Dreams,* Wakefulness-Sleep Education and Research Foundation, Del Mar, California, 1990.

National Commission on Sleep Disorders Research. *Report of the National Commission on Sleep Disorders Research,* U. S. Government Printing Office, Washington, D. C., 1992.

Reite, Martin L., M.D., Kim E. Nagel, M.D., John R. Ruddy, M.D. *The Evaluation and Management of Sleep Disorders,* American Psychiatric Press, Washington, D.C., 1990.

U. S. Congress, Office of Technology Assessment. *Biological Rhythms: Implications for the Worker,* U. S. Government Printing Office, Washington, D. C., 1991.

Index

bathing in 48
daytime vs. nighttime activity 48
effect on sleep 47
meals in 48
not set up for daytime sleep 48
regulations of 48
nursing programs 80
nursing schools 122
Nytol® 80, 125

O

obsession 119
Office of Technology Assessment
    73
offshore oil rigs 71
oil spill 53
over-the-counter drugs 45
over-the-counter medications 33
overtime
    worked prior to Challenger space
        shuttle accident 57
overtime work
    at Kennedy
        related to Challenger space
            shuttle disaster 58

P

pain syndromes 45
panic disorder 120
paper industry 71
parasomnias 34
parenthood
    and sleep 43
Parkinson's disease 91, 118
pedestrians 65

Pennsylvania Turnpike 67
peptic ulcers 26
periodic limb movement 45, 102
petroleum industry 71
phenobarbital 125
Philadelphia, Pennsylvania
    police department
        policies on shift work 60
phobia 119
physical coordination
    affected by sleep deprivation 64
physical growth
    affected by sleep 42
physician residency programs 80
physician training
    and sleep 78
physicians 76
pickets 64
Piscopo, Joseph A. 92
police
    accidents reported to 68
police officers 25
    as shift workers
        affects of sleep deprivation 60
        most frequent time of fatal
            encounters 60
polysomnography 88
post-partum depression 43
post-partum psychosis 43
post-traumatic stress disorder 120
Potsdam, New York 70
pregnancy
    and insomnia 112
    and restless legs syndrome 105
prescription drugs 45
Presidential Commission on the

About the Author

Dr. Roger Fritz writes and speaks from forty years' experience as an educator, manager, corporate executive, university president, and highly successful consultant to over 250 clients, including AT&T, Brunswick, IBM, Caterpillar, Dial, Motorola, Pizza Hut, Sara Lee, and scores of other corporations and organizations large and small. His Ph.D. is from the University of Wisconsin. He founded Organization Development Consultants in 1972. Dr. Fritz is respected throughout the country for his ability to give creative yet practical advice on how individuals and organizations can improve and grow. His challenging consulting assignments have helped hundreds of clients and many audiences benefit each year from the stimulating ideas in his live presentations. He contributes his skills in organization management and human resource development to four companies as a member of their boards of directors.

Dr. Fritz is the author of twenty-six books, monthly columns in two national magazines, video programs, software, and thirty audio cassettes. His ideas have a daily influence on how Americans increase their effectiveness.

How to Obtain Additional Copies of
Sleep Disorders: America's Hidden Nightmare

Order copies by telephone toll-free by calling:
1-800-345-0096

In Michigan and outside the U.S.:
1-616-276-5196

By FAX:
1-616-276-5197

Mail orders to:
Publishers Distribution Service
6893 Sullivan Road
Grawn, Michigan 49637
VISA and Mastercard are accepted.
Quantity discounts are available.